Patients' Law and Ethics for Nurses

A practical guide

Paul Buka

HODDER ARNOLD

PART OF HACHETTE LIVRE UK

First published in Great Britain in 2008 by
Hodder Arnold, an imprint of Hodder Education, part of Hachette Livre UK, 338 Euston Road,
London NW1 3BH

http://www.hoddereducation.com

Hodder Headline's policy is to use papers that are natural, renewable and recyclable products and
made from wood grown in sustainable forests. The logging and manufacturing processes are
expected to conform to the environmental regulations of the country of origin.

Whilst the advice and information in this book are believed to be true and accurate at the date of
going to press, neither the author[s] nor the publisher can accept any legal responsibility or liability
for any errors or omissions that may be made. In particular (but without limiting the generality of
the preceding disclaimer) every effort has been made to check drug dosages; however it is still possible that errors have been missed. Furthermore, dosage schedules are constantly being revised and
new side-effects recognized. For these reasons the reader is strongly urged to consult the drug com-
panies' printed instructions before administering any of the drugs recommended in this book.

British Library Cataloguing in Publication Data
A catalogue record for this book is available from the British Library

Library of Congress Cataloging-in-Publication Data
A catalog record for this book is available from the Library of Congress

ISBN-13   978-0-340-93881-2

1 2 3 4 5 6 7 8 9 10

Commissioning Editor:	Jo Koster/Naomi Wilkinson
Project Editor:	Clare Patterson
Production Controller:	Andre Sim
Cover Design:	Laura DeGrasse

Typeset in 10/12 AGaramond by Charon Tec Ltd (A Macmillan Company), Chennai, India
Printed and bound in Malta

What do you think about this book? Or any other Hodder Arnold title?
Please visit our website: www.hoddereducation.com

For my father – our hero

CONTENTS

AUTHOR AND CONTRIBUTORS

Paul Buka, MIHM, MSc (Crim Justice, University of Leicester), PGCE, LLB (Hons), FETC (City & Guilds), HNC (Public Admin), RN is Senior Lecturer in Adult Nursing, Thames Valley University, London, UK, with a background in law, having specialized in Healthcare Law and in Criminal Justice. He has also taught Law and Healthcare Law and Ethics in FE and HE for several years. He has publications in the area of Law and Ethics.

Kathleen Chambers, RN, RM, RMN, Cert Ed, BSc, MA is a retired Senior Lecturer of the Faculty of Health and Human Sciences, Thames Valley University, London, UK. Her specialist clinical interests are neonatal nursing and child law. She gained an MA in Child Care Law and Practice from the University of Keele. She has considerable experience of teaching Child Law and Child Protection within pre- and post-registration nurse education.

Sue Watkinson, BA, RN, OND (Hons), PGCEA, MSc, PhD is Senior Lecturer in the Faculty of Health and Human Sciences, Thames Valley University, London, UK. Her specialist clinical interest is ophthalmic nursing and she has published extensively within this field. She gained an MSc in Educational Studies and PhD in Education from the University of Surrey. She has considerable experience of teaching research, ethics and philosophy within pre- and post-registration nurse education.

PREFACE

The patient of today is more informed of their rights. Since the implementation of the Human Rights Act 1998, in 2000, the United Kingdom has seen changes, with a political drive towards a more engaged relationship between clinician and patients who are increasingly autonomous. With a rise in complaints and potential litigation, healthcare professionals should be able to recognize and safeguard these rights. Other aspects of pre-existing law as well as ethical principles which are acknowledged universally also recognize every citizen's and patient's rights.

This book does not claim to serve the function of a standard comprehensive legal textbook; rather, it aims to give the reader a grasp of the outline of the key principles which blend together law and ethics as they relate to patients' rights. Although based on English law, the author and contributors recognize that it is useful to highlight some important aspects of Scottish law where there are differences. In healthcare provision, it is no longer possible to divorce the code of professional conduct from law and ethics. Gone are the days when the nurse could claim immunity from accountability on the basis of following medical instructions.

It is hoped that by raising more awareness of patients' rights in law and ethics the professional will improve their understanding of the rationale of clinical actions.

ACKNOWLEDGEMENTS

The author would like to thank all those involved in the production process especially my commissioning editors Jo Koster and Naomi Wilkinson, also my project editor Clare Patterson.

I also acknowledge the valuable contributions from Sue Watkinson and Kathy Chambers in respect of Chapters 2 and 4. The support from my acadamic colleagues is also appreciated. I must acknowledge Philip Chika Ojiako, Laura Carlin, Sarah Lee, Davidson Chademana, and Paula Smith for kindly assisting with painstaking reviews.

On a personal note, a big thank you to all my family especially to my wife Carol, for putting up with me as always, and most importantly I must not forget my sons Alexander Lucius and Tinashe George – they have been tremendous – always there for Dad.

TABLE OF CASES

TABLE OF STATUTES

STATUTES

STATUTORY INSTRUMENTS

EU AND INTERNATIONAL LEGISLATION

1 ASPECTS OF LAW AND HUMAN RIGHTS

WHAT IS LAW?

A child's first experience of 'the law' is to do with rules and rights, likely to be ingrained in their memory as the division between 'dos' and 'don'ts.' This division plays an important part in parental guidance on what is 'acceptable' and what is deemed to be 'unacceptable' behaviour as the child grows and develops their own persona and the morality that comes with it. This process should also sow the seeds for individual morality or ethics as well as future 'respect' of authority and the law. The ethical beliefs of an individual are likely to be influenced by the values of the society in which they are nurtured. However, there are variable factors in different societies, such as religious beliefs, cultural values and the social environment, which will shape such individual values. Accepted societal ethical values, which may be common in different upbringings, may determine how individuals as nurses will view patients' rights. This is clearly demonstrable when dilemmas arise within the nurse–patient relationship and in the course of their employment.

For the patient, however, the more incapacitated they are the more likely they are to have those rights infringed or even abused. Where there is conflict or a lack of clarity, rights may, at times, need to be defined, asserted or protected – by the law. In providing care, especially for the vulnerable patient, the nurse should have nothing to fear as long as they are acting within the confines of the law; their own morality will usually guide them towards the requirements of the law although the two may be in conflict.

The nurse needs to be aware of the possibility that they are expected (whether in clinical practice or in a court of law) not only to be aware of patients' rights but also to safeguard them from others who may encroach on them. There may be situations in which colleagues or others ostensibly close to the patient may indeed undermine patient rights. Thus, it is important that the nurse be aware of how the law defines patients' rights, which include human rights, and how ethics may influence clinical decisions in both the clinical practice and how this relates to the law. As ethics is a product of society, there is therefore no doubt that ethical views continue to influence legal decisions on crucial issues such as abortion, human fertilization and organ transplant.

Law may be seen as a system of rules or regulations that aim to regulate the conduct of a group of people as well as define their competing rights and obligations. For a law to be effective, it should also have sanctions for punishing those who fail to adhere to its stipulations. The other important element is that the sources of the law should have the authority to enact it in order to give it some efficacy and meaning. It is important to note that, 'law develops continually in response to social, political and economic conditions, and any attempt to divide up its history must largely be arbitrary' (Smith, 1962, p.3). The law should be accessible to all citizens in its application and some of the characteristics of the law are that it:

- should be certain;
- has an identity;
- is also impersonal;
- is applicable to all citizens of a country as well as to a specified group of people, by creating rights and obligations.

A notable ancient codification of law by Hammurabi (c. 1792–50bc) of Mesopotamia, known as the Hammurabi's Code, was a systematic code of laws with a total of 282 articles. The aim of the code was to regulate human conduct, both in private and in public; nevertheless, this was mostly meting out justice based on an 'eye for an eye' basis. The following aspects of the code are examples of the application of this principle:

> 218. *If a physician make a large incision with the operating knife, and kill him, or open a tumour with the operating knife, and cut out the eye, his hands shall be cut off.*
> 221. *If a physician heals the broken bone or diseased soft part of a man, the patient shall pay the physician five shekels in money.*

> *229. If a builder build a house for some one, and does not construct*
> *it properly, and the house which he built fall in and kill its*
> *owner, then that builder shall be put to death.*
>
> **Code of Hammurabi**

Throughout most societies, there are ways for individuals to assert their rights as well as to seek redress. It is possible that patients, who are usually a vulnerable group, may not be aware of or able to assert such rights. Hence, it is important that nurses are aware of patients' rights. Laws usually develop in response to the needs of society and the survival of laws depends on customary usage. They may become obsolete in time through lack of use. In some nations some good laws may be seen to be immutable and act as codes or frameworks for all other laws of the system to follow, while other laws are dependent on the 'parent' law and subject to review as times move on, in any given society or within a group of people with a common interest. While most laws are promulgated by democratically elected government, laws may nevertheless be imposed from a superior order such as the dictate of an autocratic ruler. Some may also believe that all good laws should come from a divine authority through a theocratic authority. As a representative of (theocratic) authority, some rulers in the past have been known to override the rights of their subjects.

More acceptable forms of authority in a democracy are elected representatives such as government or a body of individuals. The judiciary is an instrument or arm of the government for safeguarding and defining the rights of citizens. Likewise, democratic representation is applicable to professional bodies such as the Nursing and Midwifery Council (NMC), which are professionally representative of nurses, with the power (delegated by parliament) to regulate standards of professional behaviour (NMC, 2004). Most people would also accept that in the scientific world there are accepted laws of nature, which if breached may have unsavoury consequences.

The law may be invoked, not only in defining rights, but also in creating obligations as well as providing sanctions against those who fail to comply with its dictates; the link between ethics and law is easy to see. This is demonstrable in the following case.

R v Instan [1893] 1 QB at 453

Where, D lived with her aunt, who developed gangrene in her leg and became totally dependent and unable to call for help. The defendant failed to feed or to call for medical help, even though she remained in the house and continued to eat her aunt's food. The aunt's dead body was found in the house decomposing for about a week.

It was held: that the defendant had a duty to supply her deceased aunt with sufficient food to maintain life; in addition, the death of her aunt having been accelerated due to her neglect of this duty of care.

In the same case, it was observed furthermore that nevertheless, that breach of ethical principles does not necessarily have legal implications.

> *It would not be correct to say that every moral obligation involves a legal duty; but every legal duty is founded on a moral obligation. A legal common law duty is nothing else than the enforcing by law of that which is a moral obligation without legal enforcement.*
>
> **Lord Chief Justice Coleridge, CJ at 453,**
> **R *v* Instan [1893]**

While some may consider a case such as this reprehensible morally, the courts' objective is to examine whether the defendant has broken the law.

Regarding the purpose of law, the contribution of jurists like Albert Dicey (1835–1922) to the debate on the role of the law in society has been important in establishing its (law's), pre-eminence over disciplines such as ethics. Central to his belief was the suggestion that for it to work the law should be impartial, on the basis that no one is above the law and this includes the government. His argument was that this would ensure protection of the human rights of citizens (Dicey, 1885). Certain aspects of law, mainly related to criminal law but also to other areas, such as employment law, may encroach on citizens' rights in general. In the aftermath of the Second World War, the United Nations Universal Declaration of Human Rights 1948, proclaimed by the General Assembly of the United Nations on 10 December 1948 that:

> *Everyone's right to life shall be protected by law. No one shall be deprived of his life intentionally save in the execution of a sentence of a court following his conviction of a crime for which this penalty is provided by law.*
>
> **Article 2 (1), the European Convention**
> **on Human Rights 1950**

This ensured that the emergence of human rights would be a framework for legal issues concerning rights and obligations. In the UK, the Human Rights Act 1998 received royal assent on 9 November 1998, 25 years after Britain became a signatory on 1 January 1973 of the then European Economic Community (EEC). This came into force on 2 October 2000, aiming to give effect to UK law, the rights established in the European Convention on Human Rights 1950. The relevant aspects are explored below.

SOURCES OF LAW

The laws of most countries originate from two main sources, primary sources and secondary sources.

Primary sources of law are international treaties, the European parliament, the United Kingdom (UK) parliament and assemblies (pertaining to their respective laws) as well as international treaties. These are in the form of statute law.

Secondary sources are all other multiple sources. While France for instance is a country where laws are codified, UK laws have experienced more fluidity in their development. Delegated legislation, for example by-laws, are laws made by bodies such as local authorities and quasi non-governmental organizations (Quangos) and Statutory Instruments, which is supportive legislation enabled by a parent statute from which it is derived. In addition, there are by-laws from professional bodies established by Royal Charter, such as the Nursing and Midwifery Council (NMC). Another important source is common law, in which the courts develop the legal decisions of judges. In common law, the higher the court, the more authority a case will have for binding the lower courts.

There are four main political institutions of the EU:

1. The Council of Ministers is composed of representative ministers from each member state. This is the most effective group as the law-making body of the EU.

2. The Commission is the administrative arm of the EU, and is composed of technocrats and administrators who are responsible for drafting legislation. This is the equivalent of the civil service with the function of supporting the Council of Ministers. It is, nevertheless, headed by an unelected president.

3. The Assembly, also known as the European parliament. Unlike the UK parliament, this body has no law-making powers. Its main function is to debate on topics of interest to the EU, which may be contemporary to and of interest to Europe. Its consensus-based recommendations will be the basis for recommendations or guidelines for the Council of Ministers when they legislate. They may also influence governments as they relay decisions to influence their own national parliaments. The assembly is also responsible for electing officials such as judges.

4. The European Court of Justice is the highest court in the EU, and should not be confused with the European Court of Human Rights. Sometimes known as the Court of Justice of the European Communities, it is based

in Luxembourg. While each EU state has a sovereign jurisdiction of its different legal systems, this court is responsible for adjudicating between the EU and member states or in an interstate dispute on the interpretation of European law, for example:

- between the European Commission and a member state which fails to implement a European Union Directive;
- between the European Commission and a member state which claims that the European Commission has acted beyond its legal authority;
- national courts from member states asking for clarification on the validity of specific EC legislation (subject to Article 189/EC which defines the method, extent and application of the European laws).

Judges are chosen to sit, on the basis of representation of member states, normally serving for a renewable term of six years.

The effect is that European parliament law is binding on UK legislation by virtue of joining the EU (Blair, 2005). There are three classifications of EU laws as follows:

- Regulations, which are binding to member states, and must be applied directly in their entirety.
- Directives, which must bring into line national laws, subject to an agreed timetable for the implementation. An example is the (EU) Data Protection Directive 1995, which had as its main aim protection of personal information and harmonization of privacy laws within the EU. In the UK, it resulted in the Data Protection Act of 1998.
- Decisions are the legal decisions (or case law) of the European Court of Justice. This effectively modifies the constitutional principle that parliament can make or unmake any laws it wants.

European laws are equally binding and applicable to all countries of the UK. The UK parliament may change the law and this is subject to the EU European Court of Justice's interpretation.

In addition, the European Court of Human Rights in Strasbourg was established to deal specifically with human rights issues. The Human Rights Act 1998 is now a key statute in human rights cases in the UK. Cases may be sent to this court on an appeal basis or may go directly from the UK.

All four countries of the UK have broadly similar legal systems with some variations in a few aspects in Scottish law. English law has been influenced by a combination of laws such as Anglo-Saxon laws, French law and Scottish law. Scottish law itself has also benefited from a number of sources including English law, as well as, uniquely, Roman law, following the Roman invasion of Western Europe. By comparison, English private law has stronger connections to the feudal system. The influence of the Church is more marked in Scottish law in areas such as family, succession and property laws. Finally, the work of institutional writers, such as Professor Erskine's Institutes (1730) (Erskine's Institute of the Law of Scotland, 1871; see Smith, 1962) and Viscount Stair's Institution (1773) (Stair's Institutions of the Law of Scotland; see Smith, 1962), are a unique source for Scotland, and often quoted as an authority in Scottish law.

Following the Acts of Union in 1707, the House of Lords became the final court of appeal for all cases including Scottish civil cases, with the result that English law could be applied to Scottish cases and vice versa. In criminal law, however, appeals in Scotland continue to be heard under the High Court of Justiciary sitting as the Criminal Appeal Court, which is the supreme court.

DUTY OF CARE

Breach of a duty of care may have both criminal law and tort law consequences. In criminal law, gross negligence may be included where either criminal intent or recklessness on the part of the defendant is established (see Chapter 3, The clinical environment and patients' rights). In tort law or delict in Scotland (which includes actions for clinical negligence), the court action is initiated by the wrongdoer against the victim (Elliott and Quinn, 2005). If a nurse is negligent in providing inadequate care as a result of which a patient dies, they may be prosecuted for murder if criminal intent is established. In addition, the patient or their representative may also seek damages in compensation (or 'reparation' in Scotland) for the harm they (the victim) may have suffered as a result of the wrongdoer's (defendant or defender in Scottish law) negligent actions or omissions. The aim of tort or delict is to make reparation or restitution (Scottish law) for any harm done. A patient who suffers harm as result of healthcare professional negligence is entitled to damages in compensation for personal injury.

The following landmark Scottish case established the original duty of care principle, and is still good law today in the UK as well as often being applied in other common law systems worldwide.

Donaghue v Stevenson [1932] HL All ER Rep1

The claimant had gone to a cafe with a friend, who had bought her ice cream and a drink of ginger beer. The cafe owner poured some of the drink over her ice cream and she consumed it. When she poured the rest of it she found the decomposing remains of a dead snail. The claimant became unwell as a result. She could however not claim against the manufacturer in contract law, as she had no contract with him.

Held: the claim for damages for negligence (in tort) against the manufacturer was entitled to succeed despite not having contractual rights.

The term 'duty of care' has developed with a moral effect. It is the basis of our obligations towards others with whom we may have a relationship, with the following definition being generally accepted as a foundation in tort/delict law that, 'you must take reasonable care to avoid acts or omissions which you can reasonably foresee would be likely to injure your neighbour' (Lord Atkins, at p.580, *Donaghue* v *Stevenson* HL [1932]). The principle that a manufacturer who allows a defective product to leave their possession for distribution for sale owes a duty of care to its ultimate consumer is now applicable to the healthcare relationship. In response to the question 'who is my neighbour', the House of Lords established the so-called 'neighbour principle' in the above case, 'Persons who are so closely affected by my act that I ought reasonably to have them in my contemplation as being affected when I am directing my mind to the acts or omissions which are called in question' (Lord Atkins, at p.580, *Donaghue* v *Stevenson* [1932]). This is applicable to clinical practice in that the question of duty of care may arise when there is an allegation of negligence, and where care is said to have fallen below certain specific standards. On the basis of this principle, there is little difficulty in establishing that a healthcare professional who is responsible for treating a patient owes them a duty of care not to harm them as well as to avoid omissions, which may cause them (patients) harm. As a citizen, the nurse has his or her own rights and obligations arising from the law of the land. The obligations are based on the common law duty of care that, as a provider of care, they owe to their patient.

The law of tort or delict, which deals with claims in damages for personal injury, has certain requirements that must be met before a victim of clinical negligence can raise a claim for damages in court. They are called 'hurdles' which must be overcome before negligence is established:

1. The plaintiff or victim is owed a duty of care by the particular defendant or defender (Scotland). This is to prevent unwarranted and frivolous claims which may be unrelated to the alleged injury and also to limit the claims, as the nurse cannot be expected to owe a universal duty of care to all and sundry fitting into the category of 'patient', only to those in their care.

2. The plaintiff should have proof of breach of that duty by the defendant. There must be a sufficient degree of proximity in their relationship. This could prove to be the most difficult aspect to prove.

3. The plaintiff suffered harm as a result of the alleged breach of the duty of care.

4. Did the alleged breach cause the harm in question (*a causal nexus*), i.e. in the chain of causation or affected by the actions of the defendant?

5. In the mind of the defendant, there should reasonable foreseeability (or as common sense predicts), and this pertains to the limitation of damages. This is a matter in the public interest to limit frivolous claims and prevent the floodgates opening.

A three-stage test for duty of care has been further developed by Lord Bridge, a leading judge, to cover all aspects of liability for negligence in personal injury cases, which includes clinical negligence. The law, as it stands today, is represented by a leading case, which developed the law in *Donaghue v Stevenson*; the case is *Caparo Industries plc v Dickman* [1990] 2 AC, 605, which aimed to make the law clearer as to whether:

- the plaintiff was owed a duty of care by the defendant;
- the damage or injury of the plaintiff was reasonably foreseeable;
- the relationship between the plaintiff and the defendant was sufficiently close (proximity).

The law of course recognizes the right of the defendant to counter-argue their case in their own defence (Hodgson and Lewthwaite, 2004). One example of a defence to a claim for negligence is the response that the victim themselves caused, or contributed to, the injury.

THINKING POINT

Mrs X, an 83-year-old widow on an orthopaedic trauma ward, has just had hip surgery following a fall and a resultant fractured neck of the femur. Prior to this she had lived on her own in a two bedroomed bungalow, was self-caring apart from home help once a week to help with shopping. She is not normally confused. Her daughter cannot understand why her mother died and things were not helped by the fact that the nursing care on the ward had appeared inadequate. Post-operatively her condition had deteriorated rapidly, she was not eating, was confused and she died within 10 days of the operation, as the result, among other things, of a chest infection and MRSA infection in the wound. The following concerns were brought to the hospital's attention in a letter of formal complaint, with a view to litigation.

(Continued)

1. They were not informed of the gravity of their mother's illness as each time they asked to see a doctor, they were told that 'he was busy in theatre'.
2. They often found their mother (who was by then doubly incontinent) was left soiled and unattended to under the pretext that nurses were too 'busy'.
3. There had been poor documentation with no observations done for about five days, even though the patient had developed a cough.
4. There was also no physiotherapy provided over the weekends due to staff shortages.
5. Additionally, there were concerns about their mother's nutrition, as when they visited, she was given no help with meals and left to struggle alone.

What are the issues related to the duty of care and how would you apply the three-stage test in the *Caparo* v *Dickman* case?
How would you apply the Bolam standards to this case?

HUMAN RIGHTS AND LEGAL OBLIGATIONS

Moral philosophy (examined in more detail in Chapter 2, Ethics and patients' rights) attempts to answer questions on the basis or justification of human rights. As a signatory to European legislation, the UK has now to subscribe to its laws. The Human Rights Act (HRA) 1998 was passed to give effect (in the UK) to the European Convention on Human Rights 1950, which is based on the UN declaration of Human Rights 1948 (with 59 articles on human rights). The effect is that the HRA is now applicable to both criminal and civil law (Hodgson and Lewthwaite, 2004). The most important principle embodied in this piece of legislation (Leckie and Pickergill, 2000) is that 'everyone's right to life shall be protected by the law' (Article 2, European Convention on Human Rights and Fundamental Freedoms 1950, now part of the HRA 1998, the latter being UK law).

The general categories of rights under the HRA 1998 are classified as follows:

- unqualified/absolute rights, which cannot be amended (Articles 2, 3, 4(1) and 7);
- qualified rights, which may be modified by the state in extreme circumstances, for example in a state of emergency (Articles 4(2) 5, 6 and 12);
- limited rights, which are subject to limitation by the state depending on society's needs (Articles 8, 10 and 11).

Relevant aspects of the articles also affect the way nurses deliver care to patients. Since 2 October 2000, public and local authorities have a duty to safeguard individual rights, and these can be enforced in UK courts (Makkan, 2000) under the HRA 1998. Judges also have the power to refer to parliament for clarification of the intention of legislature, if the law is uncertain. Some aspects of the HRA affecting patient care follow.

Article 2 – Right to life: Everyone's right to life shall be protected by law. No one shall be deprived of his life intentionally save in the execution of a sentence of a court following his conviction of a crime for which this penalty is provided by law.

Article 3 – prohibition of torture: No one shall be subjected to torture or inhuman or degrading treatment or punishment. Sometimes this article has been used to support cases of withdrawal of treatment. The following case came to light as an example of an alleged breach of the above article. The court's response was to consider the patient's best interests as paramount.

NHS Trust A v *M* and *NHS Trust B* v *H* [2001] Fam 348

A hospital sought permission to discontinue artificial hydration and nutrition to a patient, who in 1997 had been diagnosed as being in a 'permanent vegetative state'. The Court held that Article 2 imposed a positive obligation to give treatment where that is in the best interests of the patient – but not where it would be futile. Discontinuing treatment would not be an intentional deprivation of life under Article 2; and provided that withdrawing treatment was in line with a respected body of medical opinion, that the patient would be unaware of the treatment and not suffering, there would be no torture under Article 3.

Environmental Law Centre (2006)

Article 8 – Right to respect for private and family life: Everyone has the right to his private and family life, his home and his correspondence. There shall be no interference by a public authority with the exercise of this right except such as is in accordance with the law. This is consistent with the patient's right of autonomy to consent to treatment and informed choice.

Article 17 – prohibition of abuse of rights: Nothing in this Convention may be interpreted as implying for any State, group or person any right to engage in any activity or perform any act aimed at the destruction of any of the rights and freedoms set forth herein or at their limitation to a greater extent than is provided for in the Convention. In the first instance, the (UK) courts may make a declaration of human rights if infringement has been proven. In the latter situation, the courts may then either award damages or choose to make a declaration only if they feel that damages are not warranted. In any cases which do not fall within the remit of the 1998 Act the court will apply existing law.

For the courts, the HRA gives effect to the Convention rights by requiring UK courts to interpret the law in compatibility with this statute. UK courts also have a duty to refer the matter to parliament if there is conflict with existing legislation, in which case they must make a 'declaration of incompatibility' and apply UK legislation, even if this is in breach of European legislation (Welch in Addis and Morrow, 2005). The onus will then be on parliament to decide on amending the existing legislation in question, in order to bring it into line with European legislation. A litigant may appeal or take their case directly to the European Court of Human Rights in Strasbourg. The extent of the human rights applies to public bodies only and does not cover private organizations. While patient A in an NHS Trust hospital may be able to raise an action subject to the HRA 1998 Act, patient B in a private hospital would not be entitled to do so. The statute also covers those in employment who may wish to litigate against an employer. Thus the act creates both civil and criminal rights. Membership of the EU has eventually made it possible for the (18) rights in the HRA schedule to be enforceable in UK courts normally within three months if this is for a declaration of rights only. If, however, a complainant is seeking damages for breach of human rights, they must file the case within a year of the date of the alleged incident. A patient resorting to litigation should be aware that the time limit for litigation under the HRA varies depending on the brief (which is the document stating the facts and points of law of a client's case).

THINKING POINT

Joe works assisting the gastroenterologist, in an endoscope unit, where he has worked for the past 12 years, having been a 'G' grade for the last six years. He is aware of his responsibilities and role but recently the department has been stretched at times due to staff shortages, but they have (only just) been coping. Joe is concerned that patients may be put at risk as the Trust has now asked the ward to carry out 18 per cent more cases than the previous year, in order to meet government targets. Recently, a near miss incident highlighted some issues when a patient nearly died through aspiration; there were not enough nurses on the floor as the nurses were forced to do portering work (their only porter would otherwise not cope). A nurse looking after two patients was busy with one patient and had not noticed that the other patient had been sick and was aspirating. Fortunately, and by chance, Joe was passing when he noticed the patient's condition and reacted quickly to assist the patient, avoiding a dangerous situation.

(Continued)

1. Consider the local policy or guidelines for a similar procedure within your department.
2. If you were concerned about patient health and safety, consider how you would address this issue.
3. What is your duty of care to the patient and how does this arise in law in respect of the *Donaghue* and the *Caparo* cases?

LITIGATION AND COMPENSATION

Until the passing of the Crown Proceedings Act 1947, the crown could not be sued. Following removal of crown immunity, it is now possible for the crown to have liability in tort/delict, with a government minister having nominal liability (Cracknell, 2000) In fact, subject to Section 40(1) of that act, the Queen cannot be made personally liable in tort. In addition, judges cannot be sued for action in the process of dispensing their duties.

With modern-day advancements in medicine, patients have raised expectations (Davies, 2001). In addition, owing to current policy standards, any high expectations on quality of care may be reinforced. There are different time limits within which legal action for a personal injury claim can begin. In the case of deliberately caused personal injury, the longer window of six years from the date of injury is allowed. The most common claim in a personal injury case is for 'negligence' and the time limit for this is three years (Limitation Act 1980 or the Prescription and Limitation (Scotland) Act 1973). The effect is that court proceedings must be issued within three years in cases involving personal injury or death and six years in any other cases. Time limits start from the date on which a victim was first aware of or should have been aware of having suffered an injury (Section 11, Limitation Act 1980).

Exceptions would be made where the plaintiff had no way of knowing about the injury, or defects which are latent, for example in the case of disability where a person is suffering from a medical condition such as depression (Section 33(3) Limitation Act 1980). Another example is where a contract is carried out fraudulently and defects show up at a later date, in which case the time limit or 'prescription period' would start to run from the time of the knowledge. An example is that of the effects of a surgical operation carried out negligently.

However, it should be noted that subject to Section 33 of the Limitation Act 1980, if it appears inequitable for the courts to disallow the claim, 'the Judge has discretionary powers to disapply any time limits, and it could reasonably be argued that in view of the disabling nature of depressive illness on its subject, the Judge ought to exercise that discretion'.

A victim claiming damages must also establish (on a balance of probabilities) the facts before the courts can awards damages for personal injury in tort (McHale *et al.*, 1998). Some claims fall short of the requirements at the initial hurdles or obstacles in the stages of the claim, as it can be difficult to prove clinical negligence especially where there are latent complications of a clinical event, which may surface a long time afterwards. It has been suggested that 'only a relatively small proportion of victims of medical negligence bring an action for damages and, and approximately 76% of these failed' (Mason *et al.*, 2002, p.272). Latent claims may be allowed at the discretion of the court.

Litigation usually involves an uphill struggle and most victims cannot afford the hassle, the time and money to fight a case. In order to recover damages, a claimant must establish on a balance of probabilities that the defendant's negligence had a material effect on the outcome of the disease. Healthcare professionals who are deemed to have a specialist skill will be judged by the standards of a reasonably competent healthcare professional. The Bolam standards were first established in the Bolam case (for details of the case, see Chapter 3, The clinical environment and patients' rights). This means that a professional is judged by the standards of his peers. In order to protect patients, the courts will apply reasonable or higher standards of care, rather than lower, as the norm. The following case illustrates this point:

Wilsher v Essex Area Health Authority [1987] QB 730.CA, [1988] AC 1074

The plaintiff was born prematurely. Subsequently the defendant negligently gave the plaintiff excess oxygen. A catheter was wrongly inserted into his vein on two occasions instead of his artery and as a result, he developed an incurable eye condition. The court nevertheless accepted that his blindness could have been caused by one of any other related conditions found in premature babies. The hospital admitted negligence in general on the grounds of the doctor's actions but the court upheld the objective standard in respect of a junior doctor who could not argue his inexperience as a reason to avoid liability.
  Held, that the hospital was liable.

Davies (2001) acknowledges that there are potential difficulties in accessing evidence, which is mainly documented in clinical records. The reality of the matter is that over many years, witnesses may move, forget what happened, change their mind or may die before the case comes to court. Delays may work against a victim if key witnesses die or are untraceable. The Access to Health Records Act 1990 gives a patient or their representative the right to access non-computerized clinical records, with the Data Protection Act 1998 regulating records that are computerized.

The NHS Litigation Authority

The NHS Litigation Authority (NHSLA) was established in 1995 as part of the National Health Service (NHS), with responsibility for dealing with any claims against the NHS and acting as a kind of insurance. It is responsible for representing NHS organizations such as Trusts. It receives and manages a pool of contributions from each organization while also providing risk management by monitoring the level and the nature of claims. Available evidence suggests that the level of claims is on the rise (NHSLA, 2006).

> In 2004–05, 5609 claims of clinical negligence and 3766 claims of non-clinical negligence against NHS bodies were received by the NHSLA. This compares with 6251 claims of clinical negligence and 3819 claims of non-clinical negligence in 2003–04.
>
> £502.9 million was paid out in connection with clinical negligence claims in 2004–05. This figure includes both damages paid to patients and the legal costs borne by the NHS. In 2003–04, the comparable figure was £422.5 million. The figures for non-clinical claims are £25.1 million for 2004–05 and £10.1 million for 2003–04.
>
> **_NPSA (2006)_**

In 2001, the government introduced the National Patient Safety Authority with the aim of coordinating accident reporting, leading to improved patient safety. It also encourages an open and fair culture through such reporting and initiating 'preventative measures' (NPSA 2006).

Fault (UK) system

The main UK system of compensation for personal injury has been adversarial in that the victim is required to prove fault or negligence. From a clinical negligence victim's perspective, the process of seeking compensation for personal injury for clinical negligence can be protracted and difficult with the process to establish negligence being long and arduous. Unlike criminal law where the evidence must be proved 'beyond reasonable doubt', in tort law, which encompasses negligence claims, the plaintiff is only required to satisfy the court that there was negligence 'on a balance of probability'. The lower standard of proof is applicable to civil law cases, on a balance of probability. While a few cases will be settled out of court the reality for most people is that they will find litigation costs prohibitive and may not bother pursuing what may be a legitimate claim.

Another factor which may put off a potential litigant is the delay that may be involved since the conditional or 'no win, no fee' agreement has been introduced. The legal fees for lawyers would be around 40% plus additional court and experts' fees. The victims may still find themselves having to pay the legal costs for the other side if they lose unless they are covered by insurance. The difficulty with this scheme is that due to the financial risk factor for the victim's legal counsel, lawyers will be reluctant to take on a case unless they are guaranteed success.

The NHS Redress Scheme was introduced by the NHS Redress Act 2006, which is overseen by the NHS Litigation Authority. The scheme aims to compensate patients on low claims of up to £20 000 initially. This is expected to provide some help with patients' claims and avoid delays. It is noted that the limit set by the government is nowhere near the typical levels of damages awarded by the courts for claims in clinical negligence cases.

Other key elements of the NHS Redress Bill and Scheme include:

- *Provision for patients to receive redress in the form of care.*
- *A duty on all scheme members to appoint an appropriate person responsible for learning from mistakes.*
- *A more proactive approach to clinical negligence, with the onus no longer on the patient to initiate a claim. All scheme members will be required to review.*

DH (2005)

Systems such as those in Scandinavian countries and New Zealand have a 'no fault' system which makes it easier and quicker for the litigant; however, the damages awarded are much less than the fault system.

CONCLUSION

When aspects of the law cannot sufficiently address an issue relating to patients' rights, in ordinary civil or criminal law, the courts may also apply the HRA 1998 where appropriate. The full impact of human rights legislation has yet to be tested and is limited to public authorities, excluding patients in private care. Breach of the client's right of choice may however result in other statutory offences and as a result criminal prosecution and/or a civil action with damages for personal injury. Most patients are now more aware of their rights in general and there is a danger that in the process of asserting those rights, litigation may be seen to be the inevitable answer. When a patient becomes a victim of negligence, the trust between themselves and the healthcare professional may be eroded. The result is that where partnership and transparency should work in favour of the patient, instead there may be defensiveness and an adversarial relationship. On the other hand, because by definition most patients are defenceless, they are vulnerable. Especially when the patient lacks the capacity to assert their rights those rights may be open to abuse, even by those purportedly representing them; hence the need for criminal law to protect such patients.

What is needed is a balance between the interests of the patient and those of other stakeholders, safeguarding those of the former. Whatever reasoned decision is reached in clinical decision-making, whether it is by clinicians or by the courts, it should be in patients' best interests.

REFERENCES

Addis M, Morrow P. *Your rights, the liberty guide to human rights*. London: Pluto Press, 2005.

Blair A. *The European Union since 1945*. Harlow: Pearson Education, 2005.

Code of Hammurabi. www.lawbuzz.com/ourlaws/hammurabi/hammurabi. htm, accessed 01/06/06.

Cracknell DG (ed.). *Obligations: the law of tort*. London: Old Bailey Press, 2000.

Davies M. *Medical law*, 2nd edn. London: Blackstone Press, 2001.

Department of Health. *The NHS redress scheme*, 2005. www.dh.gov.uk/ publicationsandstatistics/pressreleases/index.htm, accessed 16/07/06.

Dicey A. *Law of the constitution, 1885*, 9th edn. London: Macmillan, 1950.

Elliott C, Quinn F. *Tort law*, 5th edn. Harlow: Pearson Longman, 2005.

Environmental Law Centre. www.elc.org.uk/pages/lawarticleshra.htm#2, accessed 23/05/06.

Hodgson J, Lewthwaite J. *Tort law*. Oxford: Oxford University Press, 2004.

Leckie D, Pickersgill D. *Human Rights Act explained*. Norwich: The Stationery Office, 2000.

Makkan S. *The Human Rights Act 1998*. London: Callow Publishing, 2000.

Mason JK, McCall RA, Laurie GT. *Law and medical ethics*, 6th edn. London: Butterworth Heinemann, 2002.

McHale J, Tingle J, Peysner J. *Law and nursing*, Oxford: Butterworth Heinemann, 1998.

NHS Litigation Authority. www.nhsla.com/home.htm, accessed 25/06/06.

NMC. *Code of professional conduct and ethics.* London: Nursing and Midwifery Council, 2004.

NPSA 2006, www.npsa.nhs.uk, accessed 25/06/06.

Smith TB. *Scotland, the development of its laws and constitution.* London: Stevens and Sons, 1962.

2 ETHICS AND PATIENTS' RIGHTS

Sue Watkinson

INTRODUCTION

In this chapter, the term 'ethics' will be considered in the same way that the meaning of the term 'law' was considered and discussed at some length in Chapter 1. Some definitions of the term 'ethics' will be offered and four main approaches to ethics will be outlined to provide the reader with a basis for understanding a subsequent and more detailed discussion on the relevance of ethics for practice. A brief review of the philosophical dimension on ethical theories provides some insight into how the concepts of 'ethical values' and 'human rights' have emerged, and enhance the reader's appreciation of the significance of the relationship between ethics and patients' rights. The areas of rights and freedom of choice, necessity and the greater good principle, ethical decision-making frameworks, and ethics and the therapeutic relationship will subsequently be discussed. Thinking points have been included to engage the reader in some ethical thinking and decision-making related to the ongoing discussion.

WHAT IS 'ETHICS'?

In its broadest context, ethics is the study of human conduct (Thompson, 2005, p.3). It is a general term for what is often described as the science of morality. Indeed, the western tradition of ethics is sometimes called moral philosophy. Thompson (2003, p.121) specifically defines 'ethics' as the study of how people behave; what they do, the reasons they give for their actions and the rationale behind their decisions. In other words, ethics implies a rational and systematic study of moral issues. Thompson (2005, p.3–4) further suggests that ethics is not simply concerned with average standards of behaviour, but rather that it is about the quest to find what is right and good, and the best way to live. It is about wanting to find a basis for the values by which to live, on the assumption that justice and happiness will follow.

Approaches to ethics

The main approaches to ethics may be categorized as:

- descriptive ethics;
- normative ethics;
- meta-ethics;
- applied ethics.

Descriptive ethics examines the moral choices and values that are held in a particular society. For example, some societies impose the death sentence for certain crimes while others do not. It is closely related to sociology and moral psychology in that it describes the way people in different societies behave. It also examines the background influences on what people do. The key feature of all descriptive ethics is that it does not examine or question issues of right or wrong. It simply states what the case is (Thompson, 2005).

Normative ethics examines the norms by which people make moral choices (Thompson, 2005). In other words, it examines issues of right and wrong, and how people justify the decisions they make when faced with situations of moral choice. Normative ethics may also be called 'moral philosophy', since it is the rational examination of morality (Thompson, 2003). It involves questions about one's own duty, in other words, what one 'ought' to do. These are referred to as deontological questions. It also asks questions about the values expressed through moral choices, in other words, what constitutes the 'good' life. These are sometimes referred to as axiological questions. Normative ethics takes a statement about behaviour and asks 'Is it right to do that?'. For example, is it right to allow euthanasia? Here, one is asking about the norms of behaviour and the basis upon which people decide right from wrong.

Meta-ethics is a discussion of the meaning of moral language and how it can be justified (Thompson, 2005). Instead of asking 'Is it right?', the question asked is 'What does it mean to say that something is right?', or 'What am I doing when I make that sort of statement?' Meta-ethics represents a response to the viewpoint that all moral propositions are meaningless. It is basically attempting to find out what people do mean (Thompson, 2005).

Applied ethics examines moral choices that are made in the light of ethical theories (Thompson, 2005).

ETHICS – ITS RELEVANCE FOR PRACTICE

From an examination of these definitions and ethical approaches, the relevance of 'ethics' for professional practice becomes clearer. It is about making judgements that are considered to be in the best interests of the individual. Applied ethics is particularly important for practising nurses as it allows the testing of ethical theories by applying them to practical situations to see whether they work and provide reasonable outcomes.

Judgement

Judgement can be viewed from many standpoints. Rowson (1990) points out that people make judgements about what is right and wrong from the standpoints of law, morality, visual taste and what is effective in practical terms. He further points out that we are all called upon to judge behaviour from the following standpoints (Rowson, 1990: 6):

- law;
- social etiquette;
- professional codes or professional etiquette;
- religious beliefs;
- visual and 'aesthetic' sense;
- what is most practical;
- morality.

For the practising nurse the most important reference viewpoint is that of the NMC Code of Professional Conduct (Nursing and Midwifery Council, 2004). For example, a nurse ought to refuse to 'accept delegated functions without first having received instruction in regard to those functions and having been assessed as competent'. For instance, a junior nurse who has been requested by a senior nurse to perform a wound dressing on a patient with a leg ulcer should refuse if she has not been previously supervised and deemed competent in the application of her knowledge of the principles of asepsis to the skill of undertaking an aseptic wound dressing.

Ethics is an integral part of decision-making within professional practice. Practising nurses are involved on a daily basis in difficult decision-making regarding the management of their patients. However, what makes this process difficult is the application of moral views since morality is becoming increasingly more complex within a multicultural, postmodern world. Coverston and Rogers (2000) point out that the latter is exemplified by complex change related to vast increases in information and technology, and exposure to diverse people and ideas. Practising nurses encounter patients from many different cultural backgrounds and this constant exposure to cultural and individual differences should heighten their awareness and knowledge of different values and beliefs.

Values

Ethical decisions are based in values, and if there is no concordance in values, or agreement as to which values take precedence over others, then a problem arises as to how to make a decision. As previously mentioned, the NMC Code of Professional Practice (Nursing and Midwifery Council, 2004) serves as a framework for decision-making. It may be regarded as an interpretative framework. In applying this concept of an interpretative framework, it might be argued that professional practice is subjective since an individual interpretation is involved, which is based on both individual and professional values and belief systems (Watkinson, 1999). As a result, practising nurses continue to encounter many ethical dilemmas that arise from a conflict between personal and professional values and beliefs. The problem is that such frameworks are protected by professional validation and are seldom questioned or challenged (Watkinson, 1999). Professional practice is underpinned by the concept of holism. However, can the practice of holistic individualized care ever become the reality when working with such professional frameworks, or do such frameworks constrain that possibility? The practising nurse is not a pure, objective and impersonal being since she is involved in the process of human judgement that can be fallible and open-ended (Watkinson, 1999). Personal confusion and dualistic thinking may result, thus negating the possibility of solving personal or professional dilemmas. However, thinking and reasoning about the moral dimensions of practice will help the development of more effective ethical decision-making skills in the best interests of patients. Consider the following scenario.

Case study

A mental health nurse working within a forensic mental healthcare setting is utilizing the Roper, Logan and Tierney model of nursing as a basis for her healthcare decision-making. She identifies the problem of poor personal hygiene in a male client displaying psychotic symptoms and with a strong tendency to aggressive and violent behaviour. The nurse knows that physical intervention to improve the client's personal hygiene by arranging for him to be physically assisted to have a bath or wash would be a correct decision to make within the guiding framework of the nursing model. However, she decides instead to simply discuss with the client the need to improve personal hygiene.

Would you consider the mental health nurse's decision-making to be right or wrong in this situation?

PHILOSOPHICAL DIMENSION ON ETHICAL VALUES AND HUMAN RIGHTS

At this stage in the discussion a brief review of the main philosophical ethical theories will provide some insight into how the concepts of 'ethical values' and 'human rights' have been formed. For the nurse practitioner, a knowledge and understanding of these concepts will further enhance an appreciation of the significance of the relationship between ethics and patients' rights.

Ethical theory is defined as 'the study of the nature and justification of general ethical principles that can be applied to moral problems, and attempts to provide a more rigorous systematic approach to how decisions are made' (Keatings and Smith, 2000, p.13). The two most common theories are teleological theory and deontological theory.

Teleological theory is also called utilitarianism or consequentialist theory. This theory was advanced by Jeremy Bentham (1748–1832), a teleological ethicist, and is about judging whether the consequences of actions are good or bad. John Stuart Mill (1806–73) also contributed to this theory by emphasizing the balance between the benefits and risks to people, associated with a certain action. Mill argued that if actions lead to the best outcome for the highest number of people, they are perceived as the best actions. The two approaches to utilitarianism either consider particular acts in relation to particular circumstances (act utilitarianism), or formulate rules of conduct that determine what is right or wrong in general (rule utilitarianism) (Keatings and Smith, 2000). Thus, decision-making about nursing practice has 'utilitarian moral justification' if it produces good consequences for the care of patients and is beneficial for the care of future patients. The NMC Code of

Professional Conduct (Nursing and Midwifery Council, 2004) is a good example of rule utilitarianism.

Both act and rule utilitarianism, however, contain flaws associated with predicting the future. Individuals can use their life experiences to attempt to predict outcomes, but no individual can be certain that his or her predictions will come true. Consider the following example:

THINKING POINT

A staff nurse was working the late shift on a male surgical ward. It was 3pm and Wayne, a 19-year-old patient, admitted for elective surgery on his left leg following a motorbike accident a few months ago, had only just arrived back from theatre. He was received by the staff nurse who was aware that Wayne had been sent to theatre early that morning having been fasted from 12 pm the previous day. A little while later, Wayne asked the staff nurse for something to eat as he was very hungry. Lunch had finished and the supper trolley was not due to arrive until 6 pm. Meanwhile Wayne was given some toast to eat. However, shortly afterwards he complained again of hunger.

The staff nurse decided to look in the ward kitchen and found a spare chicken and vegetable pie left over from lunch time. She quickly reheated the pie in the microwave oven and then served it to a grateful Wayne, who devoured it with relish. Unfortunately, 24 hours later, Wayne was beginning to show the signs and symptoms of salmonella poisoning.

From this scenario, it can be seen that despite the staff nurse's best intentions, her actions failed to benefit the patient, and in fact, caused harm and a great deal of suffering. As a professional practitioner, taking the risk of reheating a meal that had already been kept in an ambient temperature for a period of time was unethical.

Preference and interest utilitarianism

These approaches represent more modern developments of utilitarianism theory. They can also be seen to be the basis for the development of the concept of human rights since they seek to examine the 'interest' of 'preferences' of everyone concerned with a particular situation, and are very much based on the rights of and autonomy of individuals.

As Thompson (2003) points out, a key problem with utilitarian arguments is that utilitarianism itself does not define the nature of 'good'. Therefore, people might have different ideas about what constitutes their benefit, advantage or happiness in respect of their race, culture, gender or sexual orientation. However, while it is important to consider what is in people's interest, it is also important to recognize that what is in the interests of one person may not be in the interests of another. Nevertheless, within a democratic society the political situation has to reflect the right of all individuals to express their own preferences, rather than have other people's ideas of a benefit, advantage or happiness imposed on them. Preference utilitarianism was a form introduced by Hare (2001), who argued that it was important to consider individuals' preferences, except where those preferences came into direct conflict with the preferences of others. The aim is to maximize the chances of satisfying everyone's preferences.

Deontological theory

This was first associated with the moral philosophy of Immanuel Kant (1724–1804) in the late eighteenth century. Deontological theories assert that individuals have a special status, and because of that status, they are owed a respect that must not be violated regardless of consequences (Furrow, 2005). Respect for persons and their rights and duties are the building blocks of moral reasoning.

One weakness of this theory, however, is that there is no rationale or logical basis for deciding an individual's duties. Consider the following example: A student nurse may decide it is her duty always to arrive early for her college course lecture. Although this appears to be a noble duty there is no way of knowing her reasons for choosing to make this her duty. The reason perhaps could be that she always has to sit in the same chair in the front row of the classroom.

Other weaknesses of deontology include the fact that sometimes an individual's duties are in conflict, and that deontology is not concerned with the welfare of others. Consider the same example again: If the student nurse who must arrive early for her college course lecture is running late, how is she supposed to drive? Is the student nurse supposed to speed, breaking her duty to society to uphold the law, or is she supposed to arrive at her lecture late, breaking her duty to arrive early? This scenario of conflicting obligations does not lead to a clear ethically correct resolution, nor does it protect the welfare of others from the nurse's decision.

Kant's theory is in sharp contrast to utilitarianism. The demand to treat all persons as ends, not just as means, will not allow the sacrifice of individuals for the sake of the common good. Kant's theory requires a variety of duties, such as the duty to tell the truth, to keep promises and to be fair and just. Such duties must be followed independent of their consequences. Kant

argues that moral reasoning must not proceed from hypothetical imperatives, but from categorical imperatives. The hypothetical imperative is
a principle which commands us to do something only if we want to. A categorical imperative is a principle that commands us to do something independently of what we want to do. As implied from this term 'categorical'
(without conditions attached) a categorical imperative is one I must act on
under any conditions.

Pain and the individual's duties

The following examples may serve to illustrate the moral reasoning of nurses.
Research evidence suggests that post-operative pain is inadequately managed
and a difference exists between what nurses said and actually did in post-
operative pain management (Dihle et al., 2006). The most common reasons
documented for inappropriate pain management include the failure of nurses
systematically to assess and evaluate pain and its management (American
Pain Society, 1999), poor communication between nurses and patients and
limited use of a valid assessment tool (Manias et al., 2004). If the definition
of pain is taken as 'Pain is whatever the experiencing person says it is, existing
whenever s/he says it does' (McCaffery, 1983, p.14), the implication is that
there must be an appropriate response to relieve that person's pain. However,
based on the evidence, is there a case for arguing that the moral reasoning of
practitioners often proceeds from a hypothetical, as opposed to a categorical,
imperative? In other words, nurses are cognisant of the importance of effective pain management, but may not want to provide the required pain relief
due to personal fears about overdosing the patient, or encouraging addictive
behaviour and then having to encounter the consequences of their actions.
Nevertheless, the relief of pain should be a fundamental objective of any
health service (The Royal College of Anaesthetists and The Pain Society,
2003, p.1). Acute pain is common and occurs most frequently in the post-
operative period. The prescription of analgesic drugs and pain-relieving tech-
niques should be reviewed regularly to ensure that analgesia is effective and
appropriate to the level of pain experienced by the patient (The Royal
College of Anaesthetists and The Pain Society, 2003, p.4). A nurse is deemed
to act in accordance with both ethical and theoretical knowledge to enhance
competence in nursing actions related to post-operative pain management.
Failure to do so is thus morally and ethically unacceptable.

Kant argues that human beings have value, even if no one cares about
them and they are of no use to anyone. Human beings have objective worth

and must be treated with special respect. This Kantian view has substantial impact on our moral conduct. Once we recognize that human beings have objective worth, we cannot treat them merely as instruments to promote the common good, or for any other purpose.

Within the practice of caring, pain control is a contemporary ethical issue of great importance because of the devastating and dehumanizing effects pain can have on patients and their families. The deleterious effects of unrelieved acute pain are well recognized as being psychological, physiological and socio-economic in nature (The Royal College of Anaesthetists and The Pain Society, 2003, p.4). The NMC Code of Professional Conduct (Nursing and Midwifery Council, 2004) also refers to respecting patients' autonomy by identifying their preferences with regard to care. An example of this respect is illustrated when an ophthalmic nurse assesses a patient undergoing scleral buckling as a treatment modality for retinal detachment. Here, it is advisable to provide the patient with balanced information about the traumatic nature of this operative procedure and the likelihood of experiencing some persistent severe pain post-operatively. This allows the patient to make an informed decision about the type of analgesia to be administered after surgery. It is important, however, that the ophthalmic nurse does not manipulate the situation. This could result in prescribing and the administration of analgesia based on the nurse's personal preferences (hypothetical imperative). This is also ethically linked to the concept of beneficence, which promotes beneficial actions and considers the patient's best interests above the interests of the practitioner (Beauchamp and Childress, 2001).

This discussion raises two important questions as follows:

1. If practitioners agree on the need for a code of ethics, why are they failing to observe its application in daily practice, especially when planning care for those individuals who will experience severe pain following surgery?

2. Do practitioners ever consider that those decisions involving how and when to medicate for pain control fall within the domain of ethics?

These questions are worthy of reflection by practitioners in all areas of nursing practice. The concepts of ethical values and human rights have clearly emerged as an important domain from which to draw knowledge and understanding as a basis for decision-making in nursing practice.

RIGHTS AND FREEDOM OF CHOICE

Kant places great emphasis on the notion of human rights to the extent that basic freedoms are identified that have to be respected. Problems arise, however, when rights conflict. Nevertheless, a Kantian ethic asserts that rights cannot be violated simply for the sake of promoting desirable ends, whether for self or others.

The experience of freedom is an essential condition for moral choice (Thompson, 2005). However, there are limitations on freedom, and it is these limitations which often give rise to the ethical dilemmas surrounding a patient's rights and freedom of choice. Such limitations include physical, legal and social, personal and psychological, and religious. An individual cannot be morally required to do something of which he or she is physically or mentally incapable. However, for example, if an individual drinks too much alcohol and becomes physically incapable, then that individual is morally responsible for their condition and the resulting consequences. The law and society prevent individuals from doing many things as part of the overall conditioning imposed by such society. The ability to function as a mature adult may be limited by an individual's past personal and psychological experiences. Religion also influences individuals in that they may believe they are not free to oppose God's will.

Conditioning

Individuals are conditioned in various ways. There are influences on individuals' decision-making and on the moral rules that prevail in society. Conditioning equally applies to the professional community of nursing practice. If practitioners were completely free from all external causes and conditions, they would never stop to consider what they 'ought' to do, because they would never be influenced by anything that might suggest one course of action rather than another. Nurse practitioners are thus conditioned by moral rules implicit within their NMC Code of Professional Conduct (Nursing and Midwifery Council, 2004). Interaction with others is based on the four basic principles of consensus morality: non-maleficence, beneficence, justice and utility (Barker and Baldwin, 1995). These principles imply that people ought to behave in certain ways, out of a desire not to harm others, to be of positive help to others, to treat others fairly and equally, and to ensure the best possible outcome for the majority. These principles also form the basis of the belief in the autonomous person (Barker and Baldwin, 1995). As previously highlighted, respect for an autonomous person, whether self or other, is an overriding ethical principle derived from Kant.

Autonomy

To be autonomous means to be able to choose for oneself. It can be seen to operate through self-determination and self-government. Self-determination involves individuals being able to formulate and carry out their own plans, desires, wishes and policies, thereby determining the course of their own life (Barker and Baldwin, 1995, p.104). Self-government implies that as part of the notion of autonomy, individuals are able to govern their own lives by rules and values. It is also usually accepted that this involves both the mental and physical capacity to make choices and then carry them out. Most constraints on autonomy are believed to be through non-maleficence, but some may occur through benevolence. Paternalism (acting on behalf of another person in their best interest) is often used to legitimize infringement of a person's autonomy, supported by the principle of beneficence. This is the argument frequently used to impose 'treatment' on patients whether they want it or not.

THINKING POINT

Lucinda is an 83-year-old lady who has been admitted to the Care of the Elderly Mentally Ill nursing home with a diagnosis of senile dementia. Her history indicates that she has come from a very well-to-do family, and was previously accustomed to having servants in her household. She now finds herself alone with no living family members.

Lucinda has also been diagnosed with a heart condition for which she has been prescribed daily medication. During the drug round when the nursing staff ask her to take her medication, she adamantly refuses on each occasion. She says 'I don't know you; I only take medicine prescribed for me by my doctor'. Unfortunately, no amount of reassurance on the part of the nursing staff that the medication has been prescribed by her doctor will persuade her to take it. The nursing home is also situated a long way from Lucinda's home and because of this her own GP is not able to attend to provide some assistance in this situation. Because the medication is necessary, the nurses decide to crush the tablet and put it into some jam. They manage to get Lucinda to take it in this way. The nursing staff say that if the medication is not taken, the patient runs the risk of dying from her heart condition.

Do you consider it ethically acceptable to impose treatment on a patient in this way?

Nevertheless, in healthcare practice, the duty of care to protect life and health is superseded by the duty to respect autonomy. This means that competent patients have the right to refuse any form of medical intervention. Thus, it is both legally and professionally unacceptable to force treatment on competent patients because the doctor thinks it is in their best interests. The situation differs somewhat in the field of mental health practice where the effects of serious mental illness on levels of competence can sometimes reverse the moral logic of the duties of care. For instance, a mentally ill patient's capacity may become so reduced that the concept of respect for autonomy can no longer supersede protection. For example, a schizophrenic patient with delusions about being poisoned, and who is a danger to himself or to others as a result, may not understand or believe any information that contradicts this belief.

Informed consent

As previously discussed, autonomy refers to one's moral right to make decisions about one's own course of action. Thus, if the ethical principle of autonomy is applied to healthcare practice, it means that clients must be given sufficient information about healthcare prior to surgery, or other clinical interventions, and then permitted to decide for themselves about the proposed treatment. For example, before performing a gastrointestinal endoscopy, a procedure carrying considerable risk of harm, patients must give their informed consent. This involves presenting patients with the factual details, the advantages and the disadvantages of undertaking such a procedure, and the potential complications of this proposed intervention as the basis for making an informed choice. Merely disclosing information to the patient is not good enough. In order for consent to be valid, it also needs to be understood by the patient. However, questions arise about how much information needs to be disclosed to the patient before consent can be truly said to be informed. In *Sidaway* v *Board of Governors of the Bethlem Royal Hospital and the Maudsley Hospital* [1985], the law lords decided that a doctor's duty to inform a patient is an aspect of the doctor's duty to exercise reasonable care and skill. In this case, the law lords relied upon expert evidence that a body of skilled and experienced neurosurgeons would have regarded it as acceptable to warn not just of a slight but, in fact, a well-recognized risk of serious harm that Mrs Sidaway actually suffered following surgery. This case also raises the issue that the patient should have the right to choose whether to accept a slight, but well-recognized, risk of harm (Croft, 1998). Undoubtedly, there will be ongoing tension and litigation over what the reasonably competent medical practitioner regards as being significant to the making of a decision and what the typical patient regards as being important. If a medical practitioner can demonstrate that the patient's best interests were duly considered and justify any decision not to inform the patient of a risk, this is unlikely to be deemed a negligent act by the courts (Croft, 1998, p.54).

Nevertheless, informed consent should protect patients by providing complete information to make an informed decision. If the healthcare professional in performing a procedure mistakenly believes that the patient's consent has been gained, when, in fact, it has not, the healthcare professional is at risk of litigation, together with those individuals who acted as double-checkers in the situation. In these circumstances, all parties involved are liable to disciplinary proceedings by their employer (Fletcher and Buka, 1999, p.60). Thus, there exists an interface between the ethical concept and the legal doctrine of informed consent. Both are grounded in the principles of self-determination and autonomy, with disclosure being the main issue. The area of informed consent and the issues raised so far within this discussion will be expanded upon further in Chapter 5, Informed consent to treatment.

NECESSITY AND THE GREATER GOOD PRINCIPLE

In returning to the issue of autonomy, clearly the way in which consent is obtained from individual clients can raise many ethical dilemmas, in particular when individuals are not mentally competent. This applies equally to young children as well as clients of all ages whose mental state renders them unable to understand the implications of procedures or care. Specific reference has already been made to the scenario involving an elderly mentally ill patient with dementia (see Thinking point 2) which was presented for consideration of the ethical principles underpinning the decisions made. However, even where an elderly person is mentally competent to make a decision, the principle of necessity and the greater good can be applied, particularly when the individual's continued presence in a situation poses a threat to himself or herself, or to other people. In these circumstances, the principle of necessity holds good that the practitioner can use the defence that in their professional opinion, and clinical judgement, where consent cannot be obtained, the decision is taken in the best interests of the client. This is especially relevant in circumstances of life and death (see Chapter 9, End of life decisions: a matter of choice). The following example illustrates a situation where this principle could be applied with effect.

Case study

A frail, elderly lady recently widowed and now living alone in a flat on the third floor of a block of apartments has poor vision and is partially deaf. Her mobility is becoming more limited due to increasing weakness in her legs, which puts her at greater future risk of falling and sustaining injury. She has always been a fiercely independent person and is most unwilling to leave her flat and to move into a nearby nursing home for the elderly.

In this situation, a social worker is empowered by Section 47 of the National Assistance Act 1948 to have such elderly clients removed from unsuitable accommodation to a place of safety for their own sake, or that of others.

ETHICAL FRAMEWORKS AND DECISION-MAKING

There are different sources of ethical standards that can be considered to be the basis for decision-making within ethical frameworks. For the purpose of this section, five such standards are identified.

The utilitarian approach

The utilitarian approach deals with consequences. An act is morally right if, when compared with alternative acts, it yields the greatest possible balance of good consequences, or the least possible balance of bad consequences. This constitutes the principle of utility (Bloch and Green, 2006). In practical terms, it is a way of identifying the best of several alternative choices and determining whether the selected plan is the best alternative by considering the results and revising the decision accordingly (Phillips, 2006).

The rights approach

The ethical action is the one that best protects and respects the moral rights of those affected. The approach starts from the belief that humans have a dignity based on their nature or on their ability to choose freely what they do with their lives. On the basis of such dignity, they have a right to be treated as ends and not merely as means to other ends.

This approach is underpinned by the ethical concept of 'respecting persons'. This means that actions showing respect for people are morally right and actions that 'use' people are morally wrong. An individual's 'personal autonomy' (right of self-determination) must be respected, otherwise they cannot be allowed the freedom they need to be morally responsible for their actions (Rowson, 1990).

With specific reference to nursing practice, it is thought that basic physical needs, and capacities for emotional and social relationships, are an essential part of being a person. Thus, in order to respect the 'whole person' it must be accepted that an individual has a right to satisfy these needs and capacities. People have basic rights to warmth, food, shelter and sexual, emotional and social life, and such rights should be upheld as part of the general obligation to respect persons. The International Council of Nurses' Code of Ethics for Nurses (2006, p.1), as an example of an ethical framework, states 'inherent in nursing is respect for human rights, including cultural rights, the right to life and choice, to dignity, and to be treated with respect'. The NMC Code of Professional Conduct (Nursing and Midwifery Council, 2004) also documents the need to respect the beliefs, values and customs of the individual. The Code states that the autonomy of the patient should be maintained throughout treatment, restrictions being imposed only when these are demonstrably necessary for the patient's own good.

The fairness or justice approach

Within this approach, ethical actions treat all human beings equally, or, if unequally, then fairly based on some standard that is defensible. For example, access to healthcare and standard medical advice is provided free by the NHS to every citizen. However, access to an expert consultant's advice and treatment depends upon the citizen's ability to pay. In the context of healthcare practice, all patients are regarded as equally valuable regardless of their age, sex, race, colour, sexual orientation, nationality and religious or political beliefs. Thus, the well-being of each patient is considered equally important.

Plato (c.428–374BC) presents the idea that all elements in society need to work together for the general health of the whole, with the physical and assertive aspects (taken to represent the workers and defenders of society) controlled by reason (the philosophers/rulers who alone could judge what was best for society as a whole). Justice is a matter of achieving harmony among the different parts of society, and being determined and imposed by reason (Thompson, 2003, p.207). In a healthcare context, as Fletcher and Buka (1999) indicate, the principle of justice is generally held to go beyond the client as a person and to focus on the wider issues of resource management and the provision of care.

The common good approach

The Greek philosophers contributed the notion that life in a community is a good in itself and individuals' actions should contribute to that life. The approach suggests that the interlocking relationships of society are the basis of ethical reasoning and that respect and compassion for all others, especially the vulnerable, are requirements of such reasoning. It highlights the common conditions, such as the law, police and fire departments, healthcare and the education system, that are important to the welfare of all.

The virtue approach

Virtue ethics is about the virtues that make for the good life (Thompson, 2003). Examples of virtues are honesty, courage, compassion, tolerance, integrity, fairness, self-control and prudence. Virtue ethics asks of any action 'What kind of person will I become if I do this?', or 'Is this action consistent with my acting at my best?' In other words, virtues are dispositions and habits that enable individuals to act according to the highest potential of their character. Ethical actions ought to be consistent with certain ideal virtues that provide for the complete development of people.

In summary, the above approaches will help healthcare practitioners to determine what standards of behaviour can be considered ethical. However, there may be disagreement about which approaches best serve an ethical decision-making framework due to differing interpretations as to what constitutes 'good' and what constitutes 'harm'. Nevertheless, as approaches, they do provide some basis for determining what is ethical in particular circumstances. In a healthcare context, both the NMC Code of Professional Conduct (Nursing and Midwifery Council, 2004) and the ICN Code of Ethics (International Council of Nurses, 2006) embody some aspects of each of these ethical approaches to a greater or lesser extent as part of a composite decision-making framework for practice.

ETHICS AND THE THERAPEUTIC RELATIONSHIP

Currently, the focus is on the value of establishing a therapeutic relationship with patients in healthcare practice. From an ethical standpoint, engaging in a therapeutic relationship involves analysing the ethical aspects of care through competing frameworks and that engenders the concepts of patient autonomy, patient advocacy and professional autonomy.

Nursing has emphasized patient autonomy as an ethical principle, and has linked this with that of patient advocacy as a prominent aspect of professional practice (Shirley, 2007). The emphasis on the role of the nurse as advocate for the patient, the ideals of patient autonomy as an ethical guideline, and nursing's own pursuit of professional autonomy are concepts that have become part of an increasingly complex interrelationship (Shirley, 2007). Trying to establish a therapeutic relationship becomes challenging in that agreement needs to be reached with the patient in relation to establishing the balance of power across these three areas.

With specific reference to mental health practice, Hewitt and Edwards (2006) identify the ethics of care, or care-based approach, and the ethics of justice, or principle-based approach, as competing moral frameworks. They present the scenario of a schizophrenic patient found unconscious in his flat by a community psychiatric nurse, having taken an overdose of antipsychotic medication. On admission to hospital the patient states, during an interview with the nurse, that he wants to be allowed to die. However, the patient is prevented from leaving the mental health unit by virtue of his former legal status, and is placed on close observations at all times by a nurse. In trying to establish a therapeutic relationship, the problem identified is whether it is morally justified to detain the patient against his wishes in order to prevent him harming himself.

In this situation, as Hewitt and Edwards (2006) point out, the ethics of care emphasizes the value of involvement with the patient and the promotion of harmonious relationships. Sympathetic understanding is balanced by a need to respond to suicidal ideation with care and support. The care approach accepts that to act in the patient's best interests may sometimes be in conflict with the patient's wishes (Hewitt and Edwards, 2006).

The ethics of justice or principle-based approach (Beauchamp and Childress, 2001) involves four levels of moral thinking. The third level is of most significance in outlining the moral principles of respect for autonomy, non-maleficence, beneficence and justice. With this approach, obligations generated by the respect for autonomy appear to conflict with those generated by other principles. To promote the patient's well-being, nursing interventions should involve active engagement and help the patient to challenge the validity of his perceptions of hopelessness through specific problem-solving strategies and the development of future-orientated coping mechanisms (Collins and Cutliffe, 2003).

Hewitt and Edwards (2006) conclude that when the client is not capable of autonomous decision-making, the two approaches lead to the same response. When the client is capable of autonomous decision-making, the two approaches lead to different responses. From the scenario it was concluded that from a care-based perspective, intervention to prevent suicide was easier to justify and helped to formulate a nursing response as part of the therapeutic relationship.

CONCLUSION

This chapter has presented and discussed some important ethical concepts in respect of patients' rights. Ethical decision-making is a fundamental part of professional accountability. However, ethical analysis of practice is sometimes rendered very difficult in an increasingly complex moral world of competing ethical standards and frameworks. This is illustrated by the inclusion of Thinking points at appropriate stages in the discussion. It is clear that in the current climate of practice, healthcare practitioners require some knowledge and understanding of the role of ethics and its relationship with patients' rights within healthcare practice.

The focus is on working in partnership with patients, promoting their freedom of choice and maintaining their rights. This can only be achieved by a respectful consideration of the areas of patient autonomy, patient advocacy and professional autonomy and the boundaries that exist across them. Such consideration should form the basis for informed ethical decision-making for maintaining patients' rights and best interests.

REFERENCES

American Pain Society. *Principles of analgesic use in the treatment of acute pain and cancer pain*, 4th edn. Glenview, IL: American Pain Society, 1999.

Barker PJ, Baldwin S. *Ethical issues in mental health*. London: Chapman and Hall, 1995.

Beauchamp T, Childress J. *Principles of biomedical ethics*, 5th edn. New York: Oxford University Press, 2001.

Bloch S, Green S. An ethical framework for psychiatry. *British Journal of Psychiatry* 2006; **188**: 7–12.

Collins S, Cutliffe JR. Addressing hopelessness in people with suicidal ideation: building upon the therapeutic relationship utilizing a cognitive behavioural approach. *Journal of Psychiatric and Mental Health Nursing* 2003; **10**: 175–85.

Coverston C, Rogers S. Winding roads and faded signs: ethical decision making in a postmodern world. *Journal of Perinatal and Neonatal Nursing* 2000; **14**: 1–11.

Croft J. Health and human rights. A guide to the Human Rights Act 1998. London: Nuffield Trust, 1998.

Dihle A, Bjolseth G, Helseth S. The gap between saying and doing in postoperative pain management. *Journal of Clinical Nursing* 2006; **15**: 469–79.

Fletcher L, Buka P. *A legal framework for caring: an introduction to law and ethics in health care*. Basingstoke: Palgrave, 1999.

Furrow D. *Ethics. Key concepts in philosophy*. London: Continuum, 2005.

Hare RM. *The language of morals*. Oxford: Oxford University Press, 2001.

Hewitt JL, Edwards S. Moral perspectives on the prevention of suicide in mental health settings. *Journal of Psychiatric and Mental Health Nursing* 2006; **13**: 665–72.

International Council of Nurses. *ICN Code of ethics for nurses*. Geneva: ICN, 2006.

Keatings M, Smith OB. *Ethical and legal issues in Canadian nursing*, 2nd edn. Toronto: W.B. Saunders, 2000.

Manias E, Buckwell T, Botti M. Assessment of patient pain in the post-operative context. *Western Journal of Nursing Research* 2004; **26**: 751–69.

McCaffery M. *Nursing the patient in pain*. London: Harper & Row, 1983.

Nursing and Midwifery Council. *The NMC code of professional conduct: standards for conduct, performance and ethics*. London: Nursing and Midwifery Council, 2004.

Phillips S. Ethical decision-making when caring for the noncompliant patient. *Journal of Infusion Nursing* 2006; **29**: 266–71.

Rowson R. *An introduction to ethics for nurses*. London: Scutari Press, 1990.

Shirley J. Limits of autonomy in nursing's moral discourse. *Advances in Nursing Science* 2007; **30**: 14–25.

The Royal College of Anaesthetists and The Pain Society. *Pain management services – good practice*. London: The Royal College of Anaesthetists and The Pain Society, 2003.

Thompson M. *An introduction to philosophy and ethics*. London: Hodder Murray, 2003.

Thompson M. *Ethical theory*, 2nd edn. London: Hodder Murray, 2005.

Watkinson S. Tacit knowledge and professional judgement. Appraisal. *A Journal of Constructive Post-Critical Philosophy and Disciplinary Studies* 1999; **2**: 166–9.

3 THE CLINICAL ENVIRONMENT AND PATIENTS' RIGHTS

IN THE COURSE OF EMPLOYMENT

This chapter introduces the basic legal concepts related to the clinical environment and explores how this may affect not only the employer–employee relationship but also the quality of care. This may, in turn, affect patients' rights. Factors that are likely to affect the patient's 'best interests' will be considered within the contexts of professional conduct and employment law. The ethical basis of the duty of care owed to the patient will also be considered in light of professional regulations. On the premise that as an employee, a nurse freely undertakes to work for whomsoever they wish, it stands to reason that they have agreed terms and conditions of service on taking up that employment. The professional role of the nurse may be defined as follows:

> *Nursing encompasses autonomous and collaborative care of individuals of all ages, families, groups and communities, sick or well and in all settings. Nursing includes the promotion of health, prevention of illness, and the care of ill, disabled and dying people. Advocacy, promotion of a safe environment, research, participation in shaping health policy and in patient and health systems management, and education are also key nursing roles.*
>
> **International Council of Nurses (2006)**

Under normal circumstances, there is a presumption that an employer benefits from and takes credit for the positive actions of their employees (generally, the law expects that these actions will be in the course of their employment). Accordingly, it follows therefore that they (the employer) should also bear any liability resulting from the negligent actions of their employees, on the basis of 'vicarious liability'. It stands to reason, therefore, that the employer should bear the primary and ultimate responsibility for safeguarding the rights of and providing for the welfare of patients. The employer has the right to legitimately hire and fire employees, since they set out the terms and conditions of service, or ground rules, and pay the wages. In order to protect the interest of the patient, the law will therefore apportion the primary responsibility for patient care to whosoever has control of the employment activities in the caring environment, and this is the employer.

The law also presumes that the employer is liable for any actions incurred by the employee 'in the course of their employment'. In cases that have gone to law only a few decisions have gone against this general principle, and this has been when it involves employee actions 'outside the course of employment'. It is normally the employer's legal responsibility to issue terms and conditions of service to the employee, under a contract of employment, within two months of employment as regulated by the Employment Rights Act (ERA) 1996, which was amended by the Employment Relations Act (ERA) 1999 and the Employment Act 2002. If a workforce enjoys good working conditions and nurses are happy, they are likely to deliver better-quality care to patients.

Terms of employment are usually in writing although this is not necessarily the case as custom and practice may be sufficient in order to establish the terms of a contract of employment. This, however, may be difficult to prove in the event of a dispute. Where terms of a contract of employment are not written down, the court will exercise its prerogative in interpreting implied terms as shown by the relationship between an employer and employee (Phillips and Scott, 2005).

There are two of types of employment contract, a contract of services and a contract for services.

1. Contract of services is the most common type of agreement for most nurses in employment, whether full time or part time. An employee works to an agreed contract or agreement with specific terms for a specified wage or salary and this makes it easier to determine liability. However, in cases where an employee acts illegally or outside the scope of their

work, the question arises whether the employer should be made vicariously liable. The point at issue is illustrated by the following case:

Lister and Others v Hall [2001] UKHL 22

A warden who was an employee at a boarding school to look after young boys, instead abused them. The court held that although the defendant carried out criminal acts, which was not authorized by his employer, this was nevertheless, 'in the course of his employment' and therefore the employer was liable under the principle of vicarious liability.

---

2. Contract for services, on the other hand, applies to agency or hired workers who are either self-employed through an agency or working for themselves. Agency staff (who are self-employed) may face problems as there may be difficulties in establishing liability. This means that under contract law the agency may be sued for the actions of their agency worker, although this is difficult in practice unless it can be proved that they knowingly colluded with the agency nurse or acted negligently. An example of this principle is illustrated in the following case:

Dacas v Brook Street Bureau (UK) Ltd [2004] 1RLR 358

In a case where Mrs Dacas, a cleaner, who had worked on agreed hours and on a set roster as a cleaner exclusively, at a mental health hostel for Wandsworth Council for a period of 4 years. The council supplied the cleaning materials and equipment, while the agency (Brook Street) was responsible for discipline, payments to Mrs Dacas, for deductions for tax and national insurance and also for holiday and sick pay. Following allegations of alleged rudeness to a visitor, she was withdrawn from all agency work and she claimed unfair dismissal against both the council and the agency.

Held by the employment tribunal that as the claimant was not a council employee, there was no contract of employment and furthermore that there was no contract of employment between her and the agency. This decision was upheld on appeal in respect of employment by Brook Street, the agency (which was the ground for appeal), which was said to be under no obligation to provide work and there was no control over her and her work.

There is a general principle in employment law that an employer is in a financially better position than an employee. This therefore makes the employer a primary target for litigation by a victim of clinical negligence under vicarious liability. The employer is nevertheless within their rights to indemnify their own losses by suing a negligent employee, in turn as they seek recompense for any losses resulting from that employee's negligent actions, in the event of an employee acting negligently by failing to follow existing policy and procedure. In most cases nurses may also be indemnified through their union insurance for any possible mishaps. Nevertheless, if in the course of employment, it can be established that an employee was following established procedures with resulting injury to a patient, then clearly the responsibility for negligence lies with the employer. This principle was demonstrated in the case below as '…an implied term that the master will indemnify the servant from liability arising out of an unlawful enterprise upon which he has been required to embark without knowing it was unlawful'.

Lister v Romford Ice and Cold Storage Co Ltd [1957] AC 555 at 595

In this case, a truck driver while in the course of his employment as a truck driver negligently injured his father who was also an employee of the same firm. The father successfully sued the employer based on the vicarious liability principle. The employer's insurers in turn sued the driver in his capacity as joint wrongdoer and for breaching an implied term of the contract of employment, which requires of him, a duty to take reasonable care in the execution of his duties.

Since the passing of the Crown Proceedings Act 1947, the National Health Service which, as the largest employer of nurses and provider of care, had previously enjoyed an exclusion of liability under crown immunity, is now open to litigation. In the event of a patient sustaining injury through negligence of employees of the crown, government ministers or healthcare trusts, servants of the crown can now be held criminally and civilly liable in tort:

> *(1) Subject to the provisions of this Act, the Crown shall be subject to all those liabilities in tort to which, if it were a private person of full age and capacity, it would be subject:*
> *(a) in respect of torts committed by its servants or agents;*
> *(b) in respect of any breach of those duties which a person owes to his servants or agents at common law by reason of being their employer.*

Crown Proceedings Act 1947

There are, nevertheless, a few exceptions to the rule, for example the Royal Mint is immune from health and safety law, judges under qualified privilege are immune from criminal prosecution while Members of Parliament under parliamentary privilege are also immune from prosecution. The Health and Safety at Work Act 1974 (discussed below) was the precursor to the lifting of crown immunity in hospitals. This followed several incidents of food poisoning in National Health Service (NHS) establishments. The National Health Service and Community Care Act 1990 spelled the death knell of 'crown immunity', stating that:

> 1) *Subject to the following provisions of this section, on and after the day appointed for the coming into force of this subsection, no health service body shall be regarded as the servant or agent of the Crown or as enjoying any status, immunity or privilege of the Crown ... no health service body shall be regarded as the servant or agent of the Crown or as enjoying any status, immunity or privilege of the Crown.*

> **Section 60, NHS and Community Care Act 1990 (c19)**

There is now a requirement for a statutory duty of care on trusts and health providers as organizations, and making them both criminally and civilly liable for the actions or omissions of the organization as a whole. The government's vision was also included in the White Paper, *The new NHS: modern, dependable* (DoH 1997), which proposed a statutory duty for chief executives of healthcare organizations to implement systems of clinical governance to ensure good-quality care. As a result the consequence of this change has been a rise in litigation in clinical negligence actions.

> 12H (1) *it shall be the duty of each Health Board, Special Health Board and NHS trust and of the Agency to put and keep in place arrangements for the purpose of monitoring and improving the quality of health care which it provides to individuals.*

> (2) *The reference in subsection (1) to health care, which a body there mentioned provides to individuals, includes health care, which the body provides jointly with another person to individuals.*

> (3) *In this section 'health care' means services for or in connection with the prevention, diagnosis or treatment of illness.*

> **Section 51, Health Act 1999**

The NHS Redress Bill 2006 in response to the government consultation paper, Making Amends – Clinical Negligence Reform (2003) aimed at presenting the patient with an alternative to litigation for claims of less than £20,000 after deduction of medical care costs. There is no appeal and if patients are unhappy with the decision, they can institute legal proceedings unless they have accepted a settlement. There is a time limit to claims (under the Limitation Act 1980 or the Prescription and Limitation (Scotland) Act 1973; see Chapter 1, Aspects of law and human rights). Under the Employers Liability (Compulsory Insurance) Acts 1969 and 1998 (as amended by the Employers' Liability (Compulsory Insurance) (Amendment) Regulations 2004), employers are required to have insurance cover, in the event of claims. Since 1996, the National Health Service Clinical Negligence Scheme for Trusts (CNST) is the body responsible for an 'insurance policy' for any NHS clinical negligence claims.

> 4. *The Scheme applies to any liability in tort owed by a member to a third party in respect of or consequent upon personal injury or loss arising out of or in connection with any breach of a duty of care owed by that body to any person in connection with the diagnosis of any illness, or the care or treatment of any patient, in consequence of any act or omission to act on the part of a person employed or engaged by a member in connection with any relevant function of that member.*
>
> **The National Health Service (Clinical Negligence Scheme) Regulations 1996 no. 251**

THINKING POINT

John, a new junior staff nurse on Ward 'B6', which is an acute medicine for care of the elderly ward, is concerned about the problems on the ward, which has a poor reputation and a high level of complaints with the following problems:

- There is a chronic staff shortage on the ward and the ward sister says he has raised this with senior nurse managers who have not done much about it.
- Recently, he witnessed the sister and another nurse using a method which was not recommended for moving a patient but he is not sure what to do for fear of reprisals.
- There is a high incidence of MRSA on the ward and he thinks this may be linked to a generally very poor standard of hygiene on the ward.

Consider the professional issues in this case.
Consider the issue of vicarious liability from the manager's point of view.

THE HEALTH AND SAFETY OF PATIENTS AND OTHERS

The issue of safety in the care environment is important as it aims to enhance patient care. The Health and Safety at Work Act (HASAWA) (1974) is the key statute in managing risk in the area of health and safety. Section 4 of the Health and Safety at Work Act 1974 places a duty on:

> *those in control of premises, which are non-domestic and used as a place of work, to ensure they do not endanger those who work within them. This extends to plant and substances, means of access and egress as well as to the premises themselves.*
>
> **Health and Safety at Work Act 1974**

The Health and Safety Executive (HSE), through its HSE Commission, is responsible for health and safety regulation in the United Kingdom. Together with local authorities, they are the enforcing authorities and support the Commission (HSE, 2006). The employer's specific responsibilities in this area include maintaining a safe system of work as well as risk management, which includes a duty to provide appropriate equipment and appropriate staff training.

The employer is duty bound by health and safety legislation to manage risk through prevention (Ridley, 2004). For the nurse as an employee, Section 7 of the same statute requires them to take reasonable measures to ensure their own safety and that of the patient, other staff and visitors, as well as to ensure that their work is safe by avoiding risk to health to the patient, themselves, colleagues and visitors. In addition to the requirements of health and safety laws, they must also adhere to local safety policy and the instructions of their employer and report unsafe practices by colleagues. In practice it is impossible to guard against every possible eventuality in the aim to prevent harm. The courts apply the 'reasonableness' test in determining the best use of available resources in order to minimize rather than eliminate risk. In their defence, a healthcare provider, as the occupier of premises, will be required to demonstrate that they did everything reasonable, for example providing warning signs. In the event of a patient suffering harm as a result of negligence, then this may not limit liability in negligence under Section 16, Unfair Contract Terms Act 1977 if there is resulting injury or death. In all other cases strict liability applies.

There is now a legal requirement to report work-related accidents under the HSE Reporting of Injuries, Diseases and Dangerous Occurrences Regulations (RIDDOR) since the passing of the Reporting of Injuries, Diseases and

Dangerous Occurrences Regulations 1995. The classification of accidents that must be reported falls within the following categories (Croner CCH Group, 2002):

- death;
- major injuries to employees such as falls, resulting sickness of at least three days;
- other significant injury of non-employees requiring hospital treatment;
- specified diseases;
- specified dangerous occurrences including escape of noxious substances.

Health and Safety is a broad employment law concept with statutory criminal liability to ensure the protection of patients, staff and visitors. Most care is provided in designated buildings but the occupier's duty of care also extends to vehicles such as ambulances in which care may be provided. The duty of care in this area comes under what is known as 'strict liability'. The aim is to provide maximum possible protection for a 'visitor'. This includes any person present on the premises who may suffer harm. A victim does not need to prove negligence on the part of the owner of a building. Subject to the Control of Substances Hazardous to Health Regulations (COSHH) 1999, employers are required to reasonably control and protect patients, staff and visitors from exposure to hazardous substances to prevent ill health. The Ministry of Defence may be exempt under reg 17 of that statutory instrument.

The Croner CCH Group (2002, p.19) suggested the following classifications of injuries:

1. serious and disabling injuries;

2. minor injuries;

3. damage accidents;

4. accidents with no injury or near misses.

The figures for 2004/05 showed that in the workplace, which included hospitals, 220 workers were killed, a rate of 0.7 per 100 000 workers, and 361 members of the public while '150 559 other injuries to employees were reported, a rate of 587 per 100 000 employees' (HSE, 2006). However, during this period of time it is not clear how many patients died as a direct result of health and safety-related accidents. A hospital or other care provider has a duty to ensure the safe storage of hazardous substances that may injure a person coming into contact with them such as a confused patient or a child. It has been observed that the chances of a patient winning a case under health and safety legislation are better than under the normal rules of civil claim in tort (Mandelstam, 2002).

Occupier's liability – the patient and others

In land law an occupier is any person who has possession of premises, and who owns them (in the tenancy sense) and has control of activities in a building or vessel. The term 'premises' should be construed in its broadest sense, to include vehicles, for example the law protects a patient (who may be injured) while being transported in an ambulance which turns out to be defective. The rationale behind this legislation is easy to understand. Any persons entering premises should be protected from any danger, whether this is an obvious or latent defect, which may harm them. The common law creates a duty of care to ensure that they are protected. Harm should be foreseeable from the perspective of the owner of the premises. Examples of unsafe premises are those in which there is a high number of incidents involving slips, trips and falls. There are two categories of persons who can be present in premises, categorized respectively as 'visitors' and 'trespassers' as recognized by the following pieces of legislation dealing with this area:

1. The Occupier's Liability Act 1957 (OLA 1957);

2. The Occupier's Liability Act 1984 (OLA 1984).

The aim of the first statute is to create a 'common law duty of care' for the occupier to avoid harm toward persons entering the premises. The second statute, however, modified this requirement for the purpose of limiting liability where trespassers are concerned.

OLA 1957

A 'visitor' is anyone who enters the premises for a legitimate purpose. This permission to be on premises is either explicit or implied. The OLA 1957 recognizes the 'common duty of care' to visitors (Section 2(2) OLA 1957). This duty is to provide reasonable safety (Elliott and Quinn, 2005). The statute focuses on the safety of the visitor. The term 'visitor' refers to a person who is invited or has permission to be there and includes those persons who are legitimately on premises, such as patients, their visitors and the nurse; hence all are individuals who are clearly owed a duty of care. As children are assumed to be less careful than adults, the law expects higher standards of care for them, as illustrated in the following case:

> ### Glasgow Corporation v Taylor [1922] 1 AC 44, 61
>
> A 7-year-old child died after eating poisonous berries from a bush in a park owned by the Corporation. The court considered that the berries looked tempting to children since they looked like cherries. Held, that the corporation had breached their duty of care.

Subject to this statute, once injury is established, the duty of care arises on a 'strict liability' basis, with no requirement on the part of the victim to prove fault. This means that the law presumes absolute or 'strict' liability on the part of the occupier of a building. Under Section 2(4) of the same act, hospitals employing contractors may be found liable for the contractors' negligent actions (where there is defective workmanship by these contractors).

OLA 1984

The 1957 act protects only invited persons or those who are implicitly or explicitly invited by the occupier. In contrast, this statute may afford protection to those who are uninvited or trespassers, for example children who may wander on to premises are included in this category. This statute requires no strict liability unless it can be proved that the occupier (or owner of the premises) knows of or is aware of the danger, in which case the law expects them to afford reasonable protection to the trespasser. This principle is established in the following case:

> ### White v St Albans City [1990] CA
>
> This was reported in *The Times* 12 March 1990, where the claimant fell down a trench and sustained injury after he had taken a short cut across council-owned land in order to access a car park. Since the land was privately owned and surrounded by a fence, and there was no evidence that the council was aware of its use as a short cut, the Court of Appeal held on evidence that the council had taken reasonable care and were therefore not liable.

As an occupier of premises, a hospital providing healthcare is entitled to put forward certain defences to a claim for damages in tort for personal injury, for example 'contribution', which means that any damages awarded may be reduced in proportion to a victim's contribution. Another example of a defence is under the *'volenti non fit injuria'* principle (Section 2(5) of the

1957 Act), which means that the victim knowingly undertook the risk. The courts may, therefore, find for the defendant or reduce the level of damages awarded. A hospital (as occupier) may put up warning signs pointing out the danger or hazard, but cannot exclude liability under any terms of contract (Section 2(3) of the Unfair Contract Terms Act 1977) in the event of another person being killed or injured.

Manual handling and product liability

This is another important facet of health and safety legislation safeguarding the welfare of patients with mobility needs. Nurses play an important role in this process. As well as the common law duty of care based on the Health and Safety at Work Act 1974, there is a supplementary regulation on manual handling in the form of Manual Handling Operations Regulations (MHOR) 1992. The aim of any risk assessment should be 'weighing up the risk of injury against the cost or effort required to introduce new measures. Doing nothing can only be justified if the cost of measures greatly outweighs the risk' (Royal College of Nursing (RCN), 2002, p.4). Supplementary legislation operates within the framework of the HSWA 1974 (Mandelstam, 2002). The MHOR Lifting Operations and Lifting Equipment Regulations 1998 Health and Safety Commission (HSC) includes regulation of the inspection and appropriateness of equipment used for moving and handling patients.

The EC directive 85/374/EEC was passed to apply to all member states, in response to the needs of a victim facing the uphill struggle of proving negligence and product liability. Prior to the Consumer Protection Act 1987 (Product Liability) (Modification) Order 2000 and the Consumer Protection Act 1987 (Product Liability) (Modification) (Scotland) Order 2001, a plaintiff had to prove that a manufacturer was negligent before they could claim damages. Now subject to Part I of this statute, on product liability – injury caused by defective products removes the need to prove negligence providing strict liability. The causes for litigation include all defective biomedical equipment and medication, which are covered by the Consumer Protection Act 1987 above.

THINKING POINT

Jane and Jack are second year student nurses working on a busy acute surgical ward. Both of them were previously experienced healthcare assistants (level 3) prior to commencing their training and are competent at using the new hoist.

(Continued)

They are asked by the staff nurse to transfer a patient back to bed, Mrs X, who is unable to stand on her own. Both of them were competent in moving and handling patients but had not received any training on use of the new hoist. They said that they jointly made all the checks, the patient who was confused fell, sustaining a fractured neck of the femur.

1. What risk assessment should have been followed?
2. Consider your Trust's policy on reporting injuries and completing accident forms.

Infection control issues

The duty of care to patients is also applicable in cases of infection control as hospitals are required to minimize the risk by taking reasonable measures to prevent where possible or to minimize any such risk. It is a reasonable expectation in law that nurses and other healthcare professionals and workers should follow their local protocol on infection control. Negligence arises when the nurse's conduct falls below expected standards resulting in harm to patients. Either the employer or the nurse may be held to be liable, although in practice the employer is likely to be sued on the basis of vicarious liability.

> One in 10 patients who enter a British hospital will contract a nosocomial infection, and of those, 10 percent will die from it. Officially, this amounts to 5000 deaths from HAIs in the UK every year – almost double that of fatal accidents on British roads. Unofficial records show the figure to be much nearer 30 000 deaths.
>
> **Hughes and Armitage (2006)**

In order to contain an infection, patients may need to be isolated for the purpose of infection control. On the other hand, there may also be a need to balance the overall interests of all patients against those of the isolated patients. The latter may consider being isolated as a limitation of their freedom, with a possible infringement of their human rights if they feel that they have been provided a lower standard of care. The nurse is required to show that they provided a reasonable standard of care, following the principle of the *Bolam* v *Friern Barnet Hospital Management Committee* [1957] 1 WLR 582 case (the facts are discussed later in this chapter).

From the health and safety perspective, the hospital as employer has a duty of care to staff, and as occupier to patients to ensure that there are adequate resources and staffing levels when delivering care. A correlation between poor nursing staffing levels and mortality levels has in the past been confirmed by research (Aiken *et al.*, 2002; Needleman and Buerhaus, 2003). Likewise, the nurse also owes a common law duty of care to the patient and therefore a breach of that duty may give rise to a claim for damages in tort for personal injury by the patient. Given that annually, 70 000 people are estimated to die from inadequate infection control (Department of Health, 2002), it is important for Trusts to restore patient confidence in the cleanliness of ward areas. Two comparative surveys between 2002 and 2004 showed that patient ratings on cleanliness had fallen by 3 per cent from 51 to 48 per cent for 'very clean' and by 2 per cent from 41 to 39 per cent for 'fairly clean', respectively (UNISON, 2002). The Healthcare Commission may conduct unannounced visits to Trusts for inspections to ensure compliance.

ACCOUNTABILITY AND PROFESSIONAL REGULATION

The Nursing and Midwifery Council (NMC) was established under The Nursing and Midwifery Order 2001 (SI 2002/253) (the Order) and came into being on 1 April 2002. The broad principles of civil liability are addressed in more detail in Chapter 1, Aspects of law and human rights.

A very broad definition of accountability is, 'the readiness or preparedness to give an explanation or justification to relevant others (stakeholders, including the patient) for one's judgments, intentions, acts and omissions when appropriately called upon to do so' (Hunt, 2005, p.15). In practice, there is an expectation that healthcare professionals providing care will be 'accountable for the actions they take as well as their omissions' (Fletcher and Buka, 1999, p.54). The NMC expects a registered nurse, midwife or health visitor to follow this requirement: 'You are personally accountable for your practice. This means that you are answerable for your actions and omissions, regardless of advice or directions form another' (NMC Code of Professional Conduct, 2004, Clause 1.3). Nurses are also expected to give account for their actions to the following persons:

- Their professional registration body the NMC and indirectly to professional colleagues.
- The patient – those who come under the nurse's care or in the course of employment. This aims to limit reasonable foreseeability and prevent unlimited and unjustified claims should there be any claims against volunteers acting outside the scope of their work and then doing things

wrong. This is clearly a dangerous area where there is no vicarious liability and they are not indemnified by an employer or by insurance.
- The employer, under the terms of the contract of employment.

On expected standards of conduct, professionals should always turn to their own code of professional conduct for guidance. This may not always provide clear answers, especially when it comes to ethical dilemmas that professionals must deal with. At times, the professional may need to reflect on their own actions and to consider whether the patient's best interests will have been best served by their actions in a given situation. The NMC's Fitness to Practice Committee is responsible for hearing evidence with the aim of protecting the patient (and the general public in more general terms). Following a complaint from any person who has concerns on issues relating to a registrant's practice, its role is to hear the evidence, deliberate and then reach a decision which results in one of the outcomes below. The nurse will be allowed a hearing in response to any complaints. The following sanctions may be applied:

- suspending for up to a year;
- striking off;
- imposing conditions of practice;
- giving a caution order (one to five years);
- on the basis on insufficient evidence, taking no action;
- applying restricted practice.

More detailed information on the function of the NMC and its committees is available on its website www.nmc-org.uk.

Furthermore, a nurse as a professional must not only comply with the dictates of the law, which is something every citizen is required to do, but also with their professional body's codes of conduct in addition to national and local policies forming the framework for care. Wider issues on human rights may also be relevant when complaints arise. Any failure to take these into account may result in criminal prosecution, civil litigation, as well as those actions initiated by the professional body. On another level, the nurse is also accountable to the patient as well as to professional colleagues and the employer. When judging whether a nurse's standards fell below those expected, a court of law is required to ask whether, in conducting themselves in the way they did, they were acting in accordance with a practice of competent respected professional opinion (Bolam standard) or supported by evidence-based practice. The courts apply the Bolam standard thus: 'the test is the standard of the ordinary competent man (or woman) exercising and professing to have that special skill' (Justice McNair) and the facts of this case were as follows:

Bolam v Friern Hospital Management Committee [1957] 1 WLR 582

A patient suffering from endogenous depression had to undergo electric convulsive therapy. He sustained injury and multiple fractures during shock treatment, having not had a muscle relaxant administered. He sued for personal injury.

It was held that the action was entitled to fail if the professionals could show that in exercising reasonable care in carrying out the treatment they had followed a set of procedures (policies), backed by a professional body, even if there was another body of opinion with a contrary view.

The problem with the above approach, however, is that there can be difficulties when dealing with self-regulating professionals such as doctors who set their own standards (with possible accusations of 'covering each other's backs'), while purportedly protecting the patient. A more recent case echoed the standards of professional practice in Bolam:

Bolitho v City and Hackney Health Authority [1997] 3 WLR 582

A case where a doctor failed to put a tube down the throat of a child to assist his breathing. Five experts said that the doctor had been negligent and three said she had not. Lord Browne-Wilkinson ruled that only in very rare cases should a judge reject the evidence of a professional expert as being 'unreasonable', but he was entitled to do so. The majority expert evidence was admitted. The principle of this case was that it would be necessary for the court to go beyond the expertise of the alternative practitioner and to have regard to the fact that a practitioner was practising his art alongside what is generally accepted as standard or orthodox medicine.

There may nevertheless be criminal implications for negligence. The case of *R* v *Adomako* is the test for manslaughter in clinical practice.

R v Adomako [1995] 1 AC 171

An anaesthetist was assisting in an operation. At some stage during the procedure the ventilator became detached. By the time the anaesthetist became aware of this, the patient had suffered from irreversible damage and subsequently died as a result of this negligent action. The anaesthetist was convicted of manslaughter due to gross negligence as a basis for liability rather than recklessness. The test is objective, i.e. what would a reasonable person think is gross negligence. The jury considered the extent to which the defendant's conduct departed from the proper standard of care incumbent.

In order to establish clinical negligence the victim must show that the doctor, nurse or other medical attendant failed to exercise that degree of skill and care required by law and that their standard of care 'fell below the expected' (*R* v *Adomako*, 1995). The test of negligence is whether a reasonable clinician would have acted in the same way in the circumstances as the defendant nurse.

RECORD KEEPING AND COMMUNICATION

Any team of professionals needs effective communication in order to function effectively and efficiently. Communication may be defined as:

> *the exchange of information, verbally and through bodily expression between two or more people in order to influence the occurrence of action, ideas or thoughts, at work, in leisure or community pursuits or in individuals' domestic lives.*
>
> ### *Murdock and Scutt (2003)*

It has been suggested that communication involves both 'a monologue' and 'a dialogue' (Adair, 1984, p.154). Records become the outward evidence of communication. The generation and maintenance of good-quality records can be evidence of the provision of good-quality care. Multidisciplinary teams of professionals caring for the same group of patients will benefit from sharing good communication in the form of records, be it verbal or written. The latter form has, nevertheless, the advantage of being more reliable as it is permanent. Other underlying rationale for ensuring good-quality record keeping is as evidence of:

> *High standards of clinical care.*
> *Continuity of care.*
> *Better communication and dissemination of information between members of the inter-professional healthcare team.*
> *An accurate account of the treatment and care planning and delivery.*
> *The ability to detect* (and monitor) *problems, such as changes in the patient's or client's condition, at an early stage.*
>
> ### *NMC (2005, p.6)*

Owing to the importance of the nature of their work, nurses and other healthcare professionals must ensure that the quality of their work is more substantive through documentation of the relevant aspects of communication. Verbal messages may become distorted in time and depending on the people involved. Any set standards, found in both national and local guidance, must be adhered to. Many systems of work usually have their own relevant formats or templates (with certain criteria required), such as frameworks or tools for ease of information gathering, for example for carrying out nursing assessments documentation. The recording of professional activities and related communication is central to care and must therefore be informative and accurate to have any meaningful effect on care.

The importance of effective communication in nursing is underpinned by the need for professionals who are responsible for care to share information with colleagues or other healthcare professionals providing direct or indirect care. This is central to the delivery of care and essential for effectiveness and continuity. Record keeping is central to communication between the nurse and the patient as well as professional colleagues. It is therefore important that this is carried out to a high standard.

RECORD KEEPING AND THE DUTY OF CONFIDENTIALITY

A health record contains information related to a person's health, which includes both physical and mental aspects. As part of the common law duty of care to the patient the nurse must ensure that any information that identifies a patient, which comes into their hands in the course of their employment, is safeguarded and remains confidential. This principle is applied in the case of *A-G* v *Guardian Newspapers (no2) Ltd (No 2)* [1990] 1 AC 109. In a therapeutic relationship, common law as well as legislation also requires a duty of confidentiality stating that, 'patient information may not be passed on to others without the patient's consent except as permitted under Schedules 2 and 3 of the Data Protection Act 1998, or where applicable, under the common law where there is an overriding public interest' (DoH, 1996). Healthcare providers have a duty of care in ethics and in law to respect this confidentiality. Furthermore, from an ethical perspective this is not an unreasonable expectation in a fiduciary (Trust). It is also important that healthcare professionals who have access to information that may identify a patient maintain this trust-based relationship by sustaining confidentiality.

5.2 You should seek patients' and clients' wishes regarding sharing information with their family and others. When a patient is considered incapable of giving permission you should consult relevant colleagues.

NMC Code of Professional Conduct (2004)

Furthermore, in employment law, most employers will require a confidentiality clause to be included in the terms of contract of employment. This means that healthcare employees may not divulge confidential information without the risk of breaching their contract of employment.

The main statutes regulating this area are the Data Protection Act (DPA) 1988, which regulated the storage of paper (both typed and handwritten) records and the Data Protection (DPA) Act 1998 (which has largely replaced the 1984 Act and the Access to Health Records Act 1990), giving patients access to all personal data in general and electronic records specifically. Importantly, this statute also created the role of the Information Commissioner's Office (ICO) with one commissioner for England and Wales and one for Scotland. The ICO has legal powers to enforce tighter controls and to ensure that organizations comply with the requirements of the DPA 1998. It is important to note that these powers are focused on ensuring that organizations meet the obligations of the act.

The data protection powers of the ICO are to:

conduct assessments to check organisations are complying with the Act;
serve information notices requiring organisations to provide the Information Commissioner's Office with specified information within a certain time period;
serve enforcement notices and 'stop now' orders where there has been a breach of the Act, requiring organisations to take (or refrain from taking) specified steps in order to ensure they comply with the law;
prosecute those who commit criminal offences under the (DPA) Act;
conduct audits to assess whether organisations' processing of personal data follows good practice;
to report to Parliament on data protection issues of concern.

Department of Health (1996)

The Access to Health Records Act 1990 or Access to Health Records (Northern Ireland) Order 1993 used to give a patient access to their records, but has now been largely repealed and replaced by the DPA 1998, and covers only release of records in respect of deceased persons (where litigation may follow). A patient's representatives may be charged (a maximum of currently £10) for access to records. Furthermore, under the DPA 1998, a patient or their representative has free access if they wish to view records only, but must pay up to £50 for copies of manual and/or manual records. In addition, the Freedom of Information Act 2003 provides for:

> *(1) any person making a request for information to a public authority is entitled –*
> *(a) to be informed in writing by the public authority whether it holds information of the description specified in the request, and*
> *(b) if that is the case, to have that information communicated to him.*

> ### *Freedom of Information Act 2003*

Section 3 of the Public Records Act 1958 (Public Records (Scotland) Act 1937, the Public Records Act (Northern Ireland) 1923 and the Government of Wales Act 1998) allows exceptions to disclosure of records. Records may only be disclosed on three grounds:

1. if this is in the interest of public health as provided by statute;

2. for the protection of persons (including the patient) 'at risk of significant harm' NMC (2004, para 5.3);

3. when ordered to do so by a court of law.

Furthermore, subject to Section 60 of the Health and Social Care Act 2001, the Secretary of State for Health is empowered to make regulations, which authorize health service bodies to disclose information that will identify a patient. This includes data, which are patient-identifiable, if this is deemed necessary for supporting essential NHS activity or if this is in the public interest.

The principles recommended by the Caldicott Report (1997) aim at setting out the highest practical standards for handling confidential information and therefore apply equally to all routine and ad hoc flows of patient information whether clinical or non-clinical, in manual or electronic format. These must also be easily identifiable (HSC 1998/89, implementing the recommendations of the Caldicott Report).

The Caldicott Report (1997) recommended further guidance in the area of record keeping summarized in six principles:

Principle 1: Justify the purpose.

Principle 2: Do not use patient-identifiable information unless it is absolutely necessary.

Principle 3: Use the minimum necessary patient-identifiable information.
Principle 4: Access to patient-identifiable information should be on a strict need-to-know basis.
Principle 5: Everyone with access to patient-identifiable information should be aware of their responsibilities.
Principle 6: Understand and comply with the law.

These principles, combined with national and local guidance, should provide a framework of quality standards. The security and safe storage of healthcare records should be the responsibility of a locally appointed Caldicott Guardian whose responsibility is the management of confidentiality as well as access to personal information (DoH, 2001). These guidelines have since been adopted for the purpose of safeguarding public records. In addition, the requirement to respect the patient's right to privacy (Article 6 of the Human Rights Act 1998) also implies the duty of confidentiality.

CONCLUSION

It is important for nurses to demonstrate their professionalism with a high standard of record keeping as these records will serve not only as a communication tool but also as proof of the work they have done and a way to safeguard patients. Any entries, which must be factual, should be an accurate entry of events and should be clear and entered soon after the event. Another relevant requirement is the ability for the reader to identify the author, so it is important that records are clearly identifiable and signed with an identifiable designation in the case of written records (NMC, 2005). Records may be used by employers and defence lawyers as evidence in a court of law as well as by a litigant patient's counsel. The courts may take the view that if something is not written down then it did not happen, as verbal accounts of events are unreliable especially with the passage of time or due to failing human memory – events simply become more blurred or individuals may be making this evidence up.

This means that in addition to any criminal and civil liability, following a complaint, the NMC reserves the right to call to account any registered member whose conduct is alleged to have fallen below professional standards (see the case of Bolam above). Employers may also institute disciplinary procedures and/or seek damages in compensation from the employee who negligently fails to follow established local procedures (e.g. a personal injury case when the employee negligently disregards policies and procedures, inviting damages against the employee for breach of terms of a contract of employment.

Unqualified staff, on the other hand, are currently not answerable to a professional body. The primary aim of professional bodies of clinicians such as the NMC is to protect the patient's rights through professional regulation. Breach of professional regulations (misconduct) may also have legal consequences. Ethical dilemmas may arise in practice although this does not necessarily have legal or professional implications, it is almost certain that 'unethical' conduct is likely to breach the other two aspects (legal and professional). In this way, ethical dilemmas therefore present challenges for the nurse, hence the importance of working in partnership with the patient through the multidisciplinary team. The law will look sympathetically at a respondent or defendant nurse should they be able to demonstrate that they will have done everything reasonably within their power to ensure that the patient's rights are upheld. The starting point for the nurse should be to understand those aspects of employment law relating to the clinical environment, the importance of the professional code of conduct in setting standards as well as the effect of ethical values in making clinical judgements.

REFERENCES

Adair J. *The skills of leadership*. Aldershot: Gower Publishing, 1984.

Aiken LH, Clarke S, Sloane DM, Sochalski J, Silber JH. Hospital nurse staffing and patient mortality, nurse burnout, and job dissatisfaction. *JAMA* 2002; **288**: 1987–93.

Croner CCH Group. *Health and safety, A–Z, essentials.* Kingston upon Thames: Croner CG Group, 2002.

Department of Health. HSC 1998/89; Implementing the recommendations of the Caldicott Report, 1988.

Department of Health. The protection and use of patient information: guidance from the Department of Health. HSG (96)(18), 1996.

Department of Health. The Caldicott Committee Report on the Review of Patient-Identifiable Information. London: Crown Copyright, 1997. www.dh.gov.uk/prod_consum_dh/groups/dh_digitalassets/@dh/@en/documents/digitalasset/dh_4068404.pdf.

Department of Health. 2001. www.dh.gov.uk/en/Publicationsandstatistics/Publications/PublicationsPolicyAndGuidance/DH_4006467.

Department of Health. Getting ahead of the curve: a strategy for combating infectious diseases. A report by the Chief Medical Officer. London: Crown Copyright, 2002.

Department of Health. NHS confidentiality code of practice, www.doh.gov.uk.www.ico.gov.uk/what_we_cover/data_protection/legislation_in_full.aspx, 2003.

Elliot C, Quinn F. *Tort law*, 5th edn. Harlow: Pearson Longman, 2005.

Fletcher L, Buka P. *A legal framework for caring*. Basingstoke: Palgrave, 1999.

Health and Safety Executive. www.hse.gov.uk/coshh/, accessed 03/07/06.

Hughes J, Armitage T. The reformation of a national institution: combating the burden of HAIs (healthcare-associated infections): a British perspective. www.infectioncontroltoday.com/archive.html, accessed 01/07/06.

Hunt G, www.freedomtocare.org/page15.htm#definition, accessed 09/01/05.

International Council of Nurses, the ICN Code of Ethics for Nurses. www.icn.ch/definition.htm, accessed on 22/06/06.

Phillips G, Scott K. *Employment law*. Guildford: College of Law Publishing, 2005.

Mandelstam M. *Manual handling in health and social care, an A–Z of law and practice*. London: Jessica Kingsley, 2002.

Murdock A, Scutt C. *Personal effectiveness*. London: Butterworth Heinemann, 2003.

Needleman J, Buerhaus P. Nurse staffing and patient safety: current knowledge and implications for action. *International Journal for Quality in Health Care* 2003; **15**: 275–7.

Nursing and Midwifery Council. *Code of Professional Conduct. Standards for Conduct, Performance and Ethics*. London: NMC, 2004. www.nmc-uk.org.

Nursing and Midwifery Council. *Guidelines for Records and Record Keeping*. London: NMC, 2005. www.nmc-uk.org.

Ridley J. *Health and safety in brief*, 3rd edn. Burlington: Elsevier, Butterworth-Heinemann, 2004.

Royal College of Nursing. *RCN code of practice for patient handling*. London: RCN Publications, 2002.

UNISON (2002) Hospital contract cleaning and infection control, UNISON www.cf.ac.uk/socsi/CREST, accessed 10/07/06.

4 CHILDREN'S RIGHTS: THE BEGINNING OF LIFE TO THE AGE OF MAJORITY

Kathleen Chambers

This chapter will introduce the legal concepts related to children and explore the fundamental ethical and legal issues that impact on the care of children. It begins by dealing with the issues surrounding the fetus and the right to life. This is followed by the issues concerning children from birth to the age of 25 in accordance with the Children Act of 2004.

Since the beginning of 2000 many changes have taken place regarding law and ethics surrounding children which could result in dilemmas arising where nurses are not up to date or are unfamiliar with providing care for these particular clients. As today's rapidly changing healthcare market continues along its path it is leading to a generation of new issues for doctors, nurses, lawyers, judges and legislators. In this setting the rights of a child are especially challenging in relation to consent to treatment. All the rights stated in the 1989 United Nations Convention on the Rights of the Child are applicable in healthcare; however, application of the participation rights is perhaps the most challenging. Health professionals for a long time have been of the opinion that they hold power, authority and influence in their roles with children. It is very easy within child health services to substitute the word parent for patient, therefore, the rights of children are often overlooked in favour of the rights of the parents (Brook 2005). Rights, what are they and who has them? Alderson (2000) describes rights as 'equal entitlements for all members of the human family to respect their worth and dignity'. The United Nations Convention on the Rights of the Child (1989) reflects the philosophy that children too are equal, having the same inherent value as grown-ups. However, in order to have a right the person must be able to understand and comprehend that right as being theirs. Where does this leave the fetus, the preverbal child, the unconscious child, the child with learning difficulties or mental health issues? The relationship between law and ethical principles is always open to debate and examination, but where children are involved these principles present some of the most difficult, intractable and fundamental moral questions. Lee and Morgan (1991), in their book on birthrights, argued that one of the characteristics of the twentieth century was 'more clearly than any preceding century is that we have assumed the power to cause death on a hitherto undreamt of scale'. So where does that statement leave the healthcare worker?

WHEN DOES HUMAN LIFE BEGIN?

Many theories purport that the beginning of human existence as an individual is set by the moral and religious views of society and is not easily defined.

Sade (2000) argued that the issues surrounding the beginning of life existing between bioethics and law are not likely to be resolved in the foreseeable future due to the deep disagreement that persists over the questions of when does life begin. When does life end? And when does personhood begin and end? *Roe* v *Wade* 410 U.S. 113 (1973) highlights the fundamental ethical issue in abortion, arguing at what point and in what circumstances does a fetus become a person and at what point, if any, does that person have rights to an existence. The legal situation in England and Wales is that an unborn child has no legal rights, no rights at all, until birth. However, once born alive it can apply retrospective rights for criminal or civil wrongs inflicted during the pregnancy and the delivery process. This uncertainty can produce challenges for midwives, nurses and doctors when providing care and treatment options for pregnant women. This is especially so in today's climate when preterm infants born at 22–23 weeks' gestation are now surviving.

There are three pieces of legislation that affect midwives, nurses and doctors when dealing with pregnant women.

> *Every woman being with child who with intent to procure her own*
> *miscarriage, shall unlawfully administer to herself any poison or*
> *other noxious thing … or unlawfully use any instrument of other*
> *means …. And whosoever, with intent to procure the miscarriage of*

any woman whether she be or not be with child shall unlawfully administer to her any poison or other noxious thing …. Or unlawfully use any instrument or other means … shall be guilty of a felony.
The Offences Against the Person Act 1861 s.58

Any person who with intent to destroy the life of a child capable of being born alive by any wilful act causes a child to die before it has an existence independent of its mother shall be guilty of a felony … child destruction … no person shall be found guilty of an offence … unless the act which caused the death was not done in good faith for the purpose only of preserving the life of the mother.
Infant Life (Preservation) Act 1929 s.1 (1)

For the purpose of the Act evidence that a woman had at any material time been pregnant for a period of twenty eight weeks or more shall be prima facie proof that she was at that time pregnant of a child capable of being born alive.
Infant Life (Preservation) Act 1929 s.1 (2)

A person shall not be guilty of an offence under the law relating to abortion when a pregnancy is terminated by a registered medical practitioner if two registered medical practitioners are of the opinion formed in good faith.
Abortion Act 1967 (as amended by s.37 Human Fertilisation and Embryology Act 1990) s.1 (1)

These three pieces of legislation clearly identify termination of pregnancy by a registered medical practitioner with just reason not as a criminal offence, but what about the religious views? Religiously based medical ethics have a clear sense of basic values. In the Christian tradition, the belief is that human life is a divine gift, which cannot be disposed of by mortals. 'God gives and Gòd takes away' is a common belief among some religious groups. These values are translated into rules which prohibit abortion or euthanasia, such as those practised by Roman Catholic thinking. This is also linked to the belief that various forms of artificial control of fertility are morally wrong. This religious belief has led to the Abortion Act 1967 not being recognized in either the Republic of Ireland or Northern Ireland – where abortion remains illegal under Article 40.3.3 of the Constitution. However, this view is not universally supported even in the event of risk to the life of the mother, but where does this belief leave the midwife who is offering support and advice to mothers to-be-on all aspects of pregnancy, including termination of pregnancy. How can the abortion/termination issue be resolved? Many believe that it can be resolved but only if the issue of when human life begins can be determined. Marquis (2006) argued that where there is opposition to abortion the thinking is that human life begins at conception. However, those in favour of abortion argue that we will never know when human life begins. Mr Justice Harry Blackmun, writing in *Roe* v *Wade* (1973), claimed that, according to many religions and philosophies, 'life does not begin before live birth'. This is predominately the attitude of the Jewish faith and a large segment of the Protestant community. Islamic opposition is based on the concept that the fetus is not considered alive until the 40th day after conception. It is also equally based on the concept that abortion is murder. While the moderate Islamic view of ending life only when absolutely necessary is generally more universal among Muslims, a number of groups have broken off from mainstream opposition to present a more ambiguous view on themes of abortion and euthanasia (http://en.wikipedia.org/wiki/Pro-life). Blackmun further defended the view that the law has been reluctant to endorse any theory that life as we recognize it begins before live birth or to accord legal rights to the unborn. He concluded that the court had neither judicial precedent nor philosophical or theological authority for making decisions based on the judgement that life begins before live birth. If that view is true, what is the appropriate way to think of the fetus? Should we now think that the fetus is not alive until after a live delivery? This view still has the potential to create a minefield for practising midwives, in the advice they give, as the law has a legitimate interest in protecting the potentiality of human life. There are, however, certain basic rights that all humans have in virtue of being human and alive. The right to life is perhaps the most basic human right. However, if a fetus is classified as fully human and alive, then termination of pregnancy violates a basic fetal right, and is therefore wrong in the eyes of the law (Marquis, 2006).

The Abortion Act of 1967 was enacted to amend, clarify the law and remove the risk of prosecution relating to termination of pregnancy by registered medical practitioners. The act identified that a person shall not be guilty of an offence under the law when a pregnancy is terminated by a registered medical practitioner if two registered medical practitioners are of the opinion, formed in good faith, that:

- The pregnancy has not exceeded its 24th week and that the continuance of the pregnancy would involve risk greater than if the pregnancy were terminated.

- The termination is necessary to prevent grave permanent injury to the physical or mental health of the pregnant woman.
- The continuance of the pregnancy would involve risk to the life of the pregnant woman, greater than if the pregnancy were terminated.
- That there is a substantial risk that if the child were born it would suffer from such physical or mental abnormalities as to be seriously handicapped.

The Abortion Act 1967 clearly states the legal aspect but what about the moral/ethical aspect? The Nursing and Midwifery Council (NMC) professional code of conduct 2004, clause 2.4 states you must promote the interest of patients and clients, this includes helping individuals and groups gain access to health and social care, information and support relevant to their needs. Nurses and midwives have a responsibility to deliver safe and effective care based on current evidence, best practice and, where applicable, validated research. The NMC provides guidance on conscientious objection for two care areas. These are the Abortion Act 1967 (Scotland, England and Wales), which gives registrants the right to refuse to have a direct involvement in abortion procedures and the Human Fertilisation and Embryology Act 1990, which gives registrants the right to refuse to participate in technological procedures to achieve conception and pregnancy. In England and Wales registrants who conscientiously object under the above two acts are accountable for whatever decision they make and could be called upon to justify their objection within the law. In Scotland, however, the burden of proof does not rest with the objector if he or she swears an oath before a court of law explaining that he/she has an objection. However, where does this leave the nurse/midwife if her religious beliefs identify abortion/ termination of pregnancy as wrong? How can the informed advice be given in an unbiased way? Clause 2.2 of the NMC code states 'that you are personally accountable for ensuring that you promote and protect the interests and dignity of patients and clients, irrespective of gender, age, race, ability, sexuality, economic status, lifestyle, culture and religious or political beliefs'. The moral issue here lies with the professional person as it is their belief that should not be imposed on another. Nurses and midwives need to behave in a professional manner, which means that they must ensure that their beliefs are not imposed upon the client. If this means that they are unable to give the required information in an unbiased way they are required to pass the care on to another person who will be able to discuss the issue with the client in an unbiased way. Should this request be made at a booking clinic or a general practitioner's clinic it should not be a problem as there will be others around who are capable of dealing with the situation there and then. The only time that this area of care could be a problem would be when a booking appointment was being undertaken in a client's home and the professional is asked for information on terminating the pregnancy.

THINKING POINT

A young woman who appears to be 16 weeks pregnant by dates attends your clinic for the first time. She has not been seen by her general practitioner or any other health service provider and appears to have kept the pregnancy hidden. During the discussion she asks for advice on how to obtain a termination. You have made your views known to the management that you object to being directly involved in abortion procedures.

What advice could you give this client and how could you deal with her enquiry?

CHILDREN AND THE IMPACT OF LAW ON THEIR CARE

The main acts of parliament having an effect on children are the Children and Young Persons Act 1933, Children Act 1989, Family Law Act 1996, Education Act 1996, Adoption and Children Act 2002 and the Children Act 2004. The impact of these laws on children and their carers will be discussed and the factors that affect the best interest principle of the child will be considered in the context of ethics and law.

The social trends in the family have changed and continue to change with more marriages ending in divorce. More couples are living together outside marriage, more children are being born into single-parent families and more couples of the same sex are living openly together (www.statistics. gov.uk, 2006). At the same time, many family members are victims of cruel and destructive behaviour. Physical, sexual and emotional abuse continues to have a significant impact on a number of children and the numbers of victims, including children, continue to rise, therefore laws need to reflect and respond to these issues.

When the Children Act of 1989 was enacted it was seen as the most influential piece of legislation for children. Since then there have been many changes, amendments and alterations to this act and, in 2004, the new Children Act was enacted. This did not totally replace the 1989 Act as only some parts were changed, which means that now practitioners have to understand both acts as where changes were made the 2004 Act takes precedence.

With the implementation of the 2004 Act the post of a children's commissioner was established. There has been a commissioner in Wales since 2001, Northern Ireland since 2003 and Scotland since 2004. The first English commissioner was appointed in March 2005 but did not take up the post until July 2005. The general function is to promote the rights and interests of children, by 'promoting awareness of the views and interests of children'. Unlike the English commissioner, the commissioners for Wales, Scotland and Ireland are not tied by legislation to any government agenda. The commissioner for England is required to be concerned with the five outcomes set out by the government in *Every Child Matters*:

- physical and mental health and emotional well-being;
- protection from harm and neglect;
- education, training and recreation;
- the contribution made by children and young people to society;
- social and economical well-being.

Within the enactment of the Adoption and Children Act 2002 a major change, taking effect on 1 December 2003, occurred in relationship to parental responsibility. Parental responsibility is seen as a key principle and a key concept in child law and is defined in Section 3(1) to mean:

> *All the rights, duties, powers, responsibility and authority which by law a parent of a child has in relationship to the child and his/her property.*

The law has effectively thrown a ring of care around children by imposing parental responsibility for their upbringing on specific persons until the child reaches adulthood. The description of adulthood, however, has changed within the remit of the Children Act of 2004 Section 10(8).

> *A children's services authority in England and each of their relevant partners must in exercising their functions under this section have regard to any guidance given to them for the purpose by the Secretary of State. Arrangements under this section may include arrangements related to*
>
> - *persons aged 18 and 19;*
> - *persons over the age of 19 who are receiving services under Section 23C to 24D of the Children Act 1989 (c41);*
> - *persons over the age of 19 but under the age of 25 who have learning difficulties, within the meaning of Section 13 of the Learning and Skills Act 2000 and are receiving services under the Act.*

PARENTS AND PARENTAL RESPONSIBILITY

In law a mother always has parental responsibility. The position of fathers is more complicated. Section 2(1) of the Children Act 1989 states:

> *Where a child's father and mother were married to each other at the time of his birth they shall each have parental responsibility for the child.*

This statement is slightly misleading because Section 1 of the Family Law Reform Act 1987 extends this to relationships in which the parties were clearly not married at the time of birth. Parents who are involved in a void marriage are covered by Section 2(1) 'provided that at the time of the child's conception or the time of birth if later, either or both of them reasonably believed that the marriage was valid'. Added to this it is fairly common for parents who were not married at the time of the birth to marry at a later date. This arrangement is treated by the law as if they were married to each other at the time of the child's birth, and the father's status goes from one with no parental responsibility to that of full parental responsibility through the act of marrying. This act also includes the parents of adopted children; if seen as having been married at the time of the birth adopted children therefore are seen as having been born as a child of the marriage. However, what about unmarried fathers? Section 2(2) of the Children Act 1989 states:

> *Where a child's mother and father were not married to each other at the time of birth –*
>
> (a) *the mother shall have parental responsibility for the child;*
> (b) *the father shall not have parental responsibility for the child, unless he acquires it in accordance with the provisions of this Act.*

This allows mothers to enjoy all the 'rights, duties, powers, responsibilities and authorities' of being a parent with the exclusion of the father. However, the fact that fathers do not have parental responsibility does not affect any obligations they have, for example the statutory duty to maintain the child. In December 2003, after lengthy discussions which began in 1979, the Law Commission finally changed the law regarding unmarried fathers. Section 111(1) of the Adoption and Children Act 2002 made the following amendment to Section 4 of the 1989 Children Act:

> *the father shall acquire parental responsibility for the child if –*
>
> (a) *he becomes registered as the child's father under any of the enactments specified in subsection (1A);*

(b) he and the child's mother make an agreement (a parental responsibility agreement) providing for him to have parental responsibility for the child; or

(c) the court, on his application, orders that he shall have parental responsibility for the child.

Parental responsibility can be challenged and even overridden, and awarded to either grandparents or to social services, when parents and those with responsibility infringe this principle. There is no definitive list that states what are the 'rights, duties, responsibilities and authority' associated with parental responsibility, but they are seen as attributes which parents need to perform their duties properly in the rearing of their children until the children are capable of looking after themselves.

So where does this leave the professions in their daily work when dealing with issues involving children? It has and always will be easier to identify who is the mother rather than the father, when it comes to the issue of consent for treatment of a minor. Many professionals prefer the route of asking the mother to sign consent forms rather than having to ask fathers if they are married and to whom or whether they have parental responsibility for their child. This issue can be very problematic in areas such as accident and emergency, paediatrics and neonatal departments, where the child may be accompanied by fathers or carers.

THINKING POINT

You are the admitting nurse on a busy paediatric department and are dealing with a three-year-old child who has been involved in a car accident and requires immediate surgery.

You have discovered that the child is accompanied by her father and a consent form is required to be signed.

1. How would you question his parental responsibility before he signs the consent form?
2. What options are available to you if he is not married to the mother and does not have a court agreement?

CONSENT AND THE CHILD

Consent is seen as a fundamental legal and ethical right for adult patients to determine what happens to their own bodies. Valid consent to treatment is therefore absolutely central in all forms of healthcare and is seen as a matter of common courtesy between health professionals and their patients. Consent lies at the heart of the relationship between the patient and client and is a fundamental part of good practice and a legal requirement (DoH, 2001). Any adult of sound mind who is classed as a subject of the law can refuse to accept treatment irrespective of need or catastrophic outcomes. However the issue is not simple where children are involved; it is a question of what, if any, consent is required, especially in an emergency. Children in this aspect are classed as objects of the law and therefore do not have the same 'rights' as a subject of the law. The legal framework is governed in the criminal law by the law of assault and in the civil law by the duty to take reasonable care of a patient by the exercise of proper professional competence and to act in the best interests of the patient (see *Appleton* v *Garrett* BDL 2607950353; [1996] PIQR P1). Hedley (2002) argues that the real difficulties lie in the areas where consent is being refused by a child whom the clinician believes to have the capacity to consent. This is seen by many medical practitioners and nurses as a grave step to overcome and if the refusal to consent is contrary to the best interest of the child principle the decision to treat is most likely to be made by the court. (See *Re T (a minor) Wardship: Medical Treatment* BLD 2810960376; (1996) *The Times* 28 October.)

In the UK a child's 18th birthday indicates that they have reached the age of majority; this means they have finally become an adult and therefore a subject of UK law. Prior to this age children are seen as objects of the law and unable to make decisions for themselves. However in healthcare matters children of 16 to 17 years old, within a limited extent, can consent to medical treatment independently of their parents. The right of younger children to independently consent to treatment is based on their competence although a child's age is an unreliable predictor of his/her competence to make decisions. In Britain the assessment of competence is described in terms of either 'Gillick competence or the Fraser guidelines'. These are often considered to be interchangeable but in fact are quite different. Gillick competence refers to a child's capacity irrespective of age to provide valid consent to treatment in specified circumstances but not to refuse treatment. The Fraser guidelines are narrower and specifically address the issue of providing contraceptives advice to girls without the knowledge of their parents (Wheeler, 2006).

The Department of Health in November 2001 issued guidelines for professionals in obtaining consent from children, which identifies competence as a child having 'sufficient understanding and intelligence to enable him or her to understand fully what is proposed'. Since 1985 this has been referred to as 'Gillick competence'. Competence is not a simple attribute that a child possesses or does not possess; much will depend on the relationship and trust between the professional and colleagues, with the child and their family and between family members. Professionals need to work with children to develop competence by involving children from an early age in decision-making and encouraging them to take part in their care. However, where a child is under the age of 16 years it is good practice to involve the family in the decision-making. Even when children are not able to give valid consent for themselves, it is still good practice and important to involve them as much as possible in making decisions about their own health. Age-appropriate methods can be used; for example a child as young as 1 or 2 can consent to an examination of their abdomen. If when asked if you can look at their tummy, they lift up their clothes to expose their abdomen, this implies consent; however, if they put their arms around their abdomen and refuse to move them, this can be seen as no consent. For a number of years implied consent has been disregarded by the health professional due to fear of being sued for assault. However in law it is acceptable if the action by the child is documented in detail in written form, it then becomes a valid consent regarded as the same as a verbal consent. The important issue is in clear concise written documentation of the incident, which is clearly signed, timed and dated by the professional.

For consent to be valid the person, child or parent giving the consent (Department of Health, 2001) must be:

- capable of taking that particular decision which means competent;
- acting voluntarily not under any pressure or duress from anyone;
- provided with enough information to enable them to make the decision.

When gaining consent from a child it is essential that the information be provided in a form that the child can understand and that you have checked the child understands the format being used. This format could be with the use of age-appropriate language, use of pictures, toys and play activity. This information giving should be conducted at the child's own pace, allowing time and opportunity for questions concerning fears to be answered. Emergency situations are the exception to this rule. In these circumstances it is lawful to provide immediate necessary treatment and consent is not required as it is on the basis that it is in the child's best interest.

There are going to be times when children and those with parental responsibility are going to disagree with a particular investigation or treatment. The legal aspect is complex and the decisions of a competent child to accept treatment cannot be overridden by a person with parental responsibility. However, case law has decreed that when a child refuses treatment, those with parental responsibility may consent on their behalf, and treatment can lawfully be given. The Legal Capacity (Scotland) Act 1991 is broadly similar to that of England and Wales, with one important difference, in that parents cannot override a refusal of consent by a competent child. In Scotland a child under the age of 16 has the legal capacity to consent to his/her treatment where according to the Act, 'in the opinion of the qualified medical practitioner attending he/she is capable of understanding the nature and possible consequences of the procedure or treatment'.

ADVOCACY

Advocacy is about speaking up for children and young people and empowering them. Advocacy is seen to safeguard children and young people and protects them from abuse and poor practice. It makes sure that children and young people have their rights respected and their views and wishes are heard at all times. But who are the best advocates for children and young people? It is assumed by many professionals that the parents are the best advocates and that they have the best interests of their child at heart and aim to seek the best healthcare available for them. However, in agreeing to a course of action involving their child they cannot be assumed to know for certain what their preverbal child would consent to were he or she able give informed permission for an intervention. The best interest philosophy can be difficult to define with the many social, religious, philosophical and cultural ideas about what constitutes acceptable child rearing and welfare in today's multicultural society. When babies and young children are being cared for it is not always practicable to seek parents' consent on every occasion for every routine intervention such as blood or urine tests or even x-rays. However, in law, obtaining consent is a requirement. When children are admitted it is seen as good practice to discuss with the parents what routine procedures will be necessary and obtain their consent for the interventions in advance.

The Department of Health 2002 guidelines for the provision of children's advocacy services state that one of the core principles should be 'Advocates should work for children and young people and no one else'. Where does this leave the health practitioner? It is often stated and has, in some cases, become a mantra: 'I am acting as the child's advocate'. If the core principle is adhered to, this cannot be true as health service personnel are employed by a hospital and/or a community trust and therefore cannot be seen to be working for the child only. Another core principle is 'advocates should help children and young people to raise issues and concerns about things they are unhappy about' including making informal and formal complaints under Section 26 of the Children Act 1989, review of cases and inquiries into representation. If a health service employee continues along these lines and encourages a child to complain about their treatment or suggest that they have a case for suing the health authority it would have the effect of bringing them into conflict with their employing authority. By not giving true advice to the child they are not working as an advocate for the child but in the best interests of the child. This standard links to Article 12 of the United Nations Convention on the Rights of the Child 1989, which states the right of the child to express an opinion and to have that opinion taken into account, in any matter or procedure affecting the child. The General Assembly of the United Nations (UN) adopted the Convention on the Rights of the Child in November 1989 and this was implemented in English law in January 1992. Linked to this is the Human Rights Act 1998 which came into effect in October 2000. The Convention sets out a wide range of measures to safeguard and promote the physical, mental, emotional, social and behavioural development of children. This Convention recognizes that children are people who are able to form and express opinions, to participate in the decision-making process and to influence solutions and they are not merely 'adults in training'.

THINKING POINT

1. In your practice area how do you obtain consent from children and young people?
2. What support and guidance would you offer to the child and the parents/carer when a child is refusing treatment?
3. How can you support the principle of the best interest of the child in this situation?

PROTECTING THE VULNERABLE CHILD

Child abuse and neglect are generic terms encompassing all ill treatment of children including serious physical and sexual assaults as well as cases where the standard of care does not adequately support the child's health or development. Children can be abused or neglected through the infliction of harm or through the failure to act to prevent harm. Abuse can occur in a family or an institutional or community setting, such as a hospital or clinic. Significantly, a child can sustain ocular trauma and other conditions due to certain types of abuse, for example physical, sexual and neglect.

Children who are defined as being 'in need', under the Children Act 1989, which remains the same under the 2004 act, are those whose vulnerability is such that they are unlikely to reach or maintain a satisfactory level of health development, or their health and development will be significantly impaired without the provision of services (s17 (10) of the Children Act 1989). The critical factors to be taken into account in deciding whether a child is in need under the Children Act 1989 are what will happen to a child's health or development without services, and the likely effect the services will have on the child's standard of health and development. Some children may be considered as being in need because they are suffering or are likely to suffer significant harm. This is the threshold that justifies compulsory intervention in family life in the best interests of children (Children Act 1989).

Following the publication of *Working Together to Safeguard Children* (1999), *The Framework for the Assessment of Children in Need* (2000) and the Laming Report in 2003 on the death of Victoria Climbié, the issue of child protection became part of everyone's role and child protection training in the health service became a priority. Every hospital trust was given a directive that they had to identify a named doctor and nurse with specific responsibility for child protection and put in place a clear child protection policy. The Department of Health in the 1999 document had revised the four categories of child abuse and enhanced the definitions, making them clearer, with the aim of reducing the possibility of ambiguity. This still leaves the practitioner when faced with a possible child protection case to decide what constitutes an accident or a non-accidental injury. Even though the definitions have been enhanced it is still not clear-cut as to what constitutes a non-accidental injury. The Department of Health has tried to help in this area by issuing to every nurse on the NMC register a copy of the publication *What To Do If You're Worried a Child is Being Abused* (Department of Health, 2003). This document gives clear guidance on what to do, who to report to, what will happen following referral and what further contributions may be required.

Working Together to Safeguard Children (1999) sets out definitions and examples of what constitutes abuse in four categories:

1. physical abuse;

2. emotional abuse;

3. sexual abuse;

4. neglect.

Physical abuse may involve hitting, shaking, throwing, poisoning, burning or scalding, drowning, suffocating or otherwise causing physical harm to a child. Physical harm may also be caused when a parent or carer feigns the symptoms of an illness, or deliberately causes ill health to a child whom they are looking after. This situation is now commonly described using terms such as factitious illness by proxy, previously referred to as Munchausen's syndrome by proxy. In order to distinguish between accidental and non-accidental injuries and to make an informed decision practitioners need to obtain a full and comprehensive history from both the child and parents. It is the history of the coherence and timing of all the accounts of what happened that makes the difference in deciding between an accident and a non-accidental injury. One area in this category causing many problems is a parent 'hitting' a child. English law, unlike that of Scotland and Ireland, has declined to instigate a total ban on this habit. English law has allowed parents to use reasonable chastisement of their own child, without leaving a mark and without the aid of an implement. Should a mark be left this is classed as physical abuse (Children Act 2004). Practitioners need to be aware of this anomaly in the law and be able to act accordingly. Should a parent be observed chastising a child, there is a need to decide if the chastisement being used is 'reasonable' or has an implement been used which would indicate that battery has been committed, and if so the appropriate action needs to be taken to protect the child from physical abuse. Many practitioners shy away from this aspect and fail to probe and ask the difficult questions, mainly because they are unsure of what to do if the answer suggests non-accidental injury.

Emotional abuse is the persistent, emotional ill treatment of a child so as to cause severe and persistent adverse effects on the child's emotional development. It may involve conveying to children that they are worthless or unloved, inadequate or valued only insofar as they meet the needs of another person. It may feature age or developmentally inappropriate expectations being imposed on children. It may involve causing children frequently to feel frightened or in danger, or the exploitation or corruption of children. Some level of emotional abuse is involved in all types of ill treatment of a child although it may occur alone. Identification of this type of abuse is difficult and may not be obvious until teenage years or later. This may manifest itself in children being uncooperative and non-compliant especially when diagnosed with a sight problem and being prescribed 'glasses'. The practitioner may overhear the parent or carer making remarks about the child being 'ugly' with those things on their face. The child may present as being withdrawn, very quiet and have a frightened look. These signs need to be identified and reported as they may not be due to the child's fear of the unknown, such as the hospital setting, but the more sinister aspect of child abuse.

Sexual abuse involves forcing or enticing a child or young person to take part in sexual activities, whether or not the child is aware of what is happening. The activities may involve physical contact, including penetrative or non-penetrative acts. They may include non-contact activities, such as involving children in looking at, or in the production of, pornographic material or watching sexual activities, or encouraging children to behave in sexually inappropriate ways.

Neglect is the persistent failure to meet a child's basic physical and/or psychological needs, likely to result in the serious impairment of the child's health or development. It may involve a parent or carer failing to provide adequate food, shelter and clothing, failing to protect a child from physical harm or danger, or the failure to ensure access to appropriate medical care or treatment. It may also include neglect of, or unresponsiveness to, a child's basic emotional needs. This category is usually identified by observation of the child and parent interaction, but practitioners need to be aware that all neglect is not malicious. If a child is poorly dressed, but appears to be growing and well fed, it may be that the parents have a limited income and are spending the money on feeding the child. Help may be needed as these children could be classed as children in need under Section 17 of the Children Act 1989, but not necessarily suffering significant harm under Section 31 of the Children Act 1989. However, they still need to be referred to social services for help to prevent any further decline in their development. Neglect could also be identified in a case of the parent(s) not complying with the administration of eye drops, or failing to attend follow-up clinics. This type of neglect would be seen as true neglect, and the child in this case could be seen to be in danger of significant harm, without the prescribed treatment being administered correctly. Again, these cases do need to be referred to social services for help and guidance.

HANDLING DISCLOSURE INFORMATION ABOUT CHILD ABUSE

Having read about protecting the vulnerable child and looking at the four categories of abuse, the reader is probably asking the question how do we handle a disclosure? Although the information may come from a child, teenager or even an adult the guidelines are exactly the same. There is no time limit on a person disclosing child abuse and the information is treated in the same way regardless of the age of the person.

If a child/young person/adult disclosed to you that they have been abused:

- Stay calm and listen to what is being said.
- Take what is being said seriously, regardless of the age of the person.
- Reassure the child/young person/adult, but do not agree to keep the information secret.
- Allow the claimant to talk about the situation but do not pressurize them for more information.
- Try to get another person to listen to the disclosure; this is good practice as the child/young person/adult may deny the conversation, if they still feel threatened by the abuser.
- Report the incident if appropriate, remain with the child/young person/ adult, discuss the situation with a senior manager/member of staff.
- Follow your local policy and procedure, make sure that the conversation is recorded in a written format. The written report needs to identify exactly what has been said to you, not your interpretation of what had been said. Write the report clearly and factually and if appropriate get the child/young person/adult to read what you have written and sign it. This provides further evidence and is seen as good practice by the legal profession.
- Report to social services, usually by telephone, and follow this up in writing within 48 hours.
- Social services acknowledge receipt of the referral and decide on the action to be taken, within one working day.

CONCLUSION

This chapter has identified the significant current laws and changes related to paediatric practice that clearly provide major challenges for practitioners in the future. The impact of changes in the law, diagnosis, treatment and delivery of paediatric care is now being seen across all areas, whether it be in health or social care. The expansion of the National Health Service and private provision has resulted in more children being identified between the ages of 19 and 25 years, as cited in the Children Act 2004, and this will have a huge impact on the future planning requirements for the provision of facilities for children's services. The implementation of the NHS Frameworks and *Every Child Matters* will impart a fundamental change in thinking about the law, health and social care services, hopefully leading to a cultural shift concerning the delivery of services. This should therefore produce a seamless service which allows transferral from child to adult services making it as painless as it can be for the child, family and/or carers. In order to support these children through the changes, practitioners in all areas now need a sound professional knowledge and understanding of child development and the law surrounding children. It is hoped that this chapter has increased the reader's understanding and demystified some of the conceptions which surround the law, and will form the basis for a broader outlook on their own practice areas.

REFERENCES

Alderson P. *Young children's rights: exploring beliefs, attitudes, principles and practice*. London: Jessica Kingsley Publications, 2000.

Brook GD. Challenges and outcomes of working from a rights based perspective. *Archives of Diseases in Childhood* 2005; **90**: 176–8.

Department of Health. *What to do if you're worried a child is being abused*. London: Stationery Office, 2003.

Department of Health. *National standards for the provision of children's advocacy services*. London: Stationery Office, 2002.

Department of Health. *Seeking consent working with children*. London: Stationery Office, 2001.

Department of Health. *Assessing children in need and their families: practice guidelines*. London: Stationery Office, 2000.

Hedley M. Treating children: Whose consent counts? *Current Paediatrics* 2002; **12**: 463–4.

Lee R, Morgan D. *Birthrights: law and ethics at the beginning of life*. London: Routledge, 1990.

Marquis D. Abortion and the beginning and end of human life. *Journal of Law, Medicine and Ethics* 2006; **34**: 16–25.

Nursing and Midwifery Council. *Code of professional conduct standards for conduct, performance and ethics*. London: Stationery Office, 2004.

Sade RM. Introduction defining the beginning and end of human life: implications for ethics, policy and law. *Journal of Law, Medicine and Ethics* 2006; **34**: 6–7.

Wheeler R. Gillick or Fraser? A plea for consistency over competence in children. *BMJ* 2006; **332**: 807.

5 INFORMED CONSENT TO TREATMENT

ELEMENTS OF CONSENT

The concept of consent goes to the core of ethics and the issues of human freedom and autonomy to make decisions. This includes the ability to make informed choices about our lives and any necessary treatment. A patient receiving care may be in a vulnerable position if their judgement is impaired in some way. This means that there should be no presumption that blanket consent to all forms of treatment is present once the patient is receiving treatment. It is, therefore, an important aspect of communication that, in normal circumstances, before any treatment, the nurse is very clear that the patient has consented to any treatment given. One example is in invasive procedures such as inserting a nasogastric tube or giving an enema. The necessity and validity of consent raises moral issues not only about the patient's autonomy but also about the expected beneficence and non-maleficence of the nursing actions, which includes ensuring that consent is properly obtained. Any undue influence will invalidate that consent (Doyal, 2002). Consent may be classified as:

- expressed: written or oral;
- implicit;
- general;
- specific.

Expressed consent

This type of consent involves a clear expression by the patient of their wishes. Expressed consent must be explicit or the patient must be given the opportunity to openly express their agreement to the operation or examination and this may be either written or verbal.

> 2. *Consent is often wrongly equated with a patient's signature on a consent form. A signature on a form is evidence that the patient has given consent, but is not proof of valid consent. If a patient is rushed into signing a form, on the basis of too little information, the consent may not be valid, despite the signature. Similarly, if a patient has given valid verbal consent, the fact that they are physically unable to sign the form is no bar to treatment. Patients may, if they wish, withdraw consent after they have signed a form: the signature is evidence of the process of consent-giving, not a binding contract.*
>
> **Department of Health (2001a)**

Consent may be written or verbal. Both forms are valid although for evidence it is obviously better for consent to be in writing as it may be difficult to establish verbal consent. The use of a witness would be the only way of establishing this, should evidence of past consent need to be proved in a court of law. Problems may arise as a witness may forget the events, their recollection of events may change, they may move away to another job or may have died by the time a case comes to court. There is in fact no legal requirement for express consent to be in writing as the patient may be unable to write but have the capacity to consent.

> *For the consent to be valid, the patient must:*
>
> * *be competent to take the particular decision;*
> * *have received sufficient information to take it;*
> * *not be acting under duress.*
>
> **Department of Health (2001a)**

Implicit consent

The presence of consent can also be established by inference of the conduct of the patient although there may be difficulties in establishing this in retrospect. This may also be open to abuse if treatment is provided on the erroneous assumption that the patient has given permission for treatment or examination, hence it is important that the nurse should establish the fact that a patient is in agreement for a treatment intervention to go ahead. An example is when a patient sees a nurse with a syringe injection and they offer their hand as a sign that they are in agreement with the procedure being carried out. The American case below (which is only persuasive and not binding in the UK) illustrates this point.

O'Brien v *Cunard SS Co* (1891) 28 N.E 266

In this case an individual (on the defendant's ship) had stood in the queue and offered her arm for vaccination, and then subsequently testified that she did not wish to be vaccinated and had not given her consent. The courts held that there was implied consent – by willingly standing in the queue and offering her arm, and accordingly in a similar instance treatment would be justified.

A similar defence for a clinician may be allowed in court if they acted in the belief that the patient had been able to give consent by actively taking steps in acceptance of any treatment offered. The courts would also accept the use of reasonable intervening actions, which would be supported by the Bolam standards of practice (see Chapter 1, Aspects of law and human rights).

General consent

This aspect covers possible 'blanket' agreements for treatment to go ahead. The danger is that this may be open to challenge should the patient be given treatment without understanding it, or under false pretences. Although this sounds valid from a contractual point of view, there is the possibility of abuse with the patient's rights being overridden under Article 3, Human Rights Act (HRA)1998. It is, however, useful in a laparoscopy-type operation where the surgeon has the option to pursue either an alternative course of action or a more extensive operation should the outcome turn out to be different from that expected, as shown in the following case. It is possible that in the course of an exploratory operation a surgeon may find a condition other than the one he expected, which requires a more extensive operation. The patient should be warned of this possibility so that they may give consent prior to surgery. The implication of giving blanket consent is that clinicians cannot give any guarantee that the patient's rights will be ensured. In ordinary circumstances, informed consent must be obtained before any treatment. Exceptions to the rule are clearly laid out in Department of Health (2001b).

Specific consent

Any consent given by a patient must be related to the specific treatment or procedure without the discretion of the nurse to choose a completely different alternative, which may not have been agreed to by the patient. The following case illustrates this point.

Williamson v East London & City Health Authority (1997)

Lloyd's Law Reports Medical is the authority for the view that a patient should be informed of the nature and extent of the proposed treatment or surgery. The plaintiff had previously been given silicone gel breast implants at the age of 30 for cosmetic reasons and subsequently developed multiple lumps, which the surgeon associated with a leak from the silicone implant. The plaintiff having consented to breast surgery silicone replacement and lump excision only was nevertheless given instead a more radical operation. Having developed multiple lumps, a radical mastectomy operation was performed, without her consent. The court found that there had been no prior explanation by the surgeon and that the patient had not consented to the extensive surgery. She was awarded damages of £20 000 for the pain and suffering as a result of the 'negligent' action in failing to obtain consent to the operation performed.

CONSENT AND THE PATIENT'S RIGHTS

The concept of paternalism has been at the centre of traditional medicine and nursing, with the patient being a small player and not questioning clinical judgements being on the receiving end. However difficulties and ethical issues arise when doctors and nurses start to impose their own values on others who may not share them (Campbell *et al.*, 2001). The general public is now more aware of rights and has access to information from sources such as the media and the Internet. More recently, Article 8 (1) of the HRA 1998 asserts that, 'everyone has the right to respect for his private and family life, his home and his correspondence'. This article gives individuals some 'moral autonomy' (Hoffman and Rowe, 2003, p.183). Thus, for the nurse, safeguarding the patient's autonomy and their entitlement to self-determination through consent to treatment is important.

> *In a treatment setting 'informed' refers to the choice of useful therapies, usefulness being a professional decision. The informing process needs a good relationship between patient and doctor. In a research setting the principles are also generally agreed: The risks must not be*

disproportionate; and the patient (or guardian in some psychiatric settings) has to give informed consent. The first applies also where consent is not possible but here, determinations of risks and of benefits to self and others have to have the protection of the law.

WHO (2003)

Within a therapeutic relationship, the patient has a right to informed consent before treatment. This means that a sufficient degree of information must be given to allow them to make a balanced judgement as to whether to accept treatment or not. The role of the nurse should be to facilitate this process for the patient by empowering them to make decisions affecting their treatment. It is possible that a patient may not wish to receive such information but, nevertheless, the nurse must provide the patient with that opportunity to seek any clarification for treatment and the opportunity to give consent or to decline treatment.

The issue of autonomy has been at the heart of the debate for philosophers such as Immanuel Kant (1724–1804), who recognized that people have a natural right to choose because they have a free will (the categorical imperative), which every thinking human being is assumed to have by nature. Others, such as John Stuart Mill (1806–73), have also suggested that autonomy is a natural human freedom of the expression of one's opinion as well as to live in a way that expresses 'individuality' (Mill, 1993). The ethical basis of autonomy is the right to 'respect' a person's right to self-determination (Blackburn, 2001). This principle is applicable to the treatment environment, that is allowing the patient to choose treatment, and this was recognized in law in the following landmark case.

Schloendorff v *Society of New York Hospital*, 211 NY, 105 NE 92, 93 (1914), 106 N.E. 93 (N.Y. 1914)

This was a case where a woman had consented to an abdominal examination under anaesthesia but not to a surgical operation. Knowing this to be the case the surgeon went ahead to operate and remove a tumour. The patient sued for battery. Justice Cardozo's opinion (p.304) expressed what has now become the foundation for the concept of informed consent and for an individual patient's right of autonomy and self-determination: 'Every human being of adult years and sound mind has a right to determine what shall be done with his own body; and a surgeon who performs an operation without his patient's consent commits an assault for which he is liable in damages.'

Autonomy is a basic human right in ethics and in law, and this is central to consent as human beings have the capacity to weigh the facts before them and make a considered choice (Furrow, 2005). Following the above legal principle, autonomy is also seen as the ability or capacity to weigh the options and then choose moral alternatives (Thompson *et al.*, 2000). The patient has a basic right to autonomy, which is defined in law. When this right is infringed, it is therefore the patient's prerogative to choose to accept or to decline treatment, knowing that the consequences may be detrimental to their health. For the injured party (the patient), infringement of such a right may give rise to an action for damages in tort against another person who is alleged to have violated that right (Fletcher and Buka, 1999). This right is nevertheless not absolute and it is for the courts to define based on the statutory provisions as interpreted in pre-existing case law. There is also a presumption in law that all adults are competent unless proven otherwise. For individuals who are competent the patient's right to decline treatment regardless of the possible adverse outcome is recognized in common law as illustrated in the *St George's Healthcare National Health Service Trust* v *S (No 2)* reported in *The Times Law Report* of 3 August 1998. A patient also has the right to withdraw any previously given consent.

THE CLINICAL RELATIONSHIP – INFORMATION AND CAPACITY

The relationship between the nurse and their patient is based on trust and a need for purposeful and effective communication. As part of this communication process it is normal that most patients may wish to ask questions related to their treatment. The nurse has a duty in the Kantian sense to ensure that the patient's autonomy is respected. In addition, other ethical principles such as beneficence requires the promotion of good while nonmaleficence focuses on avoiding any action which may be detrimental to the patient's health (by denying them their freedom of choice) and within the Beauchamp and Childress framework (2001). The Department of Health (2001c) guidelines are clear about the clinician's responsibility for obtaining consent and for empowering the patient. It is now possible for a specially trained member of the multidisciplinary team, who is not carrying out the procedure, to obtain consent from the patient:

1. The health professional carrying out the procedure is ultimately responsible for ensuring that the patient is genuinely consenting to what is

being done: it is they who will be held responsible in law if this is challenged later.

2. Where oral or non-verbal consent is being sought at the point the procedure will be carried out, this will naturally be done by the health professional responsible. However, teamwork is a crucial part of the way the NHS operates, and where written consent is being sought it may be appropriate for other members of the team to participate in the process of seeking consent.

Where there is lack of consent there is the possibility of litigation for negligence and civil actions for trespass to the person (including assault and battery). Assault is putting another person in a state of fear for their safety and battery involves unwarranted physical contact. Carrying out procedures without consent may amount to battery or assault. Where a patient is detained in hospital against their wishes this may amount to false imprisonment unless the Mental Health Act 1983 is applied. Assault and battery may be subject to criminal prosecution under the Offences against the Person Act 1861 and other statutes.

To be able to provide adequate information, the clinician should be capable of performing or understand the nature of the procedure which the patient will undergo (Department of Health, 2001). The patient should be given a sufficient degree of information, options and the related benefits and any risks involved. For instance, where a surgical operation is concerned, the law expects a surgeon to inform the patient about the benefits and risks of a procedure. In order to enable patients to make an informed choice the standard of care is decided by the *Bolam* case: 'standard of a reasonable skilled person who professes to have those skills' and the law will judge a professional by the standard of a 'reasonable' nurse.

A clinician must always look to their own professional code of conduct as well as to local policies and guidelines for guidance. The patient must be given a sufficient degree of information to enable them to make an informed choice about whether to consent to the treatment or procedure. A doctor does not have to disclose all the risks (Giliken and Bethwith, 2004). The Bolam principle was applied in the case of *Sidaway* v *Bethlem Royal Hospital Governors* [1985] AC 871, where the plaintiff had a chronic neck condition and the surgeon recommended an operation. The surgeon failed to warn the patient of a small risk (1 per cent) as the operation was within less than 3 cm of the spinal cord. The outcome of the operation resulted in severing of the spine, causing paralysis. The patient said that she would not have agreed to the operation had she known the risk. The House of Lords held that as the risk was minimal, autonomy was not absolute and that the patient is not always the best judge on the level of information to be given. On the basis of this case it could be argued that in this instance it was effectively accepted that sometimes paternalism might be justifiable. In contrast, the case of *Hester* v *Ashfar* [2004] UKHL41 went the other way, adopting a patient-focused approach, that affirmed the patient's right to be informed of any avoidable risk, no matter how minor.

As a professional, the nurse has a duty to protect their patient's right to autonomy. For patients who are incompetent or lack capacity there is an expectation that nurses will advocate for these patients:

> *3 As a registered nurse, midwife or specialist community public health nurse, you must obtain consent before you give any treatment or care.*
>
> *3.1 All patients and clients have a right to receive information about their condition. You must be sensitive to their needs and respect the wishes of those who refuse or are unable to receive information about their condition. Information should be accurate, truthful and presented in such a way as to make it easily understood. You may need to seek legal or professional advice or guidance from your employer, in relation to the giving or withholding of consent.*
>
> *3.2 You must respect patients' and clients' autonomy – their right to decide whether or not to undergo any health care intervention – even where a refusal may result in harm or death to themselves or a foetus.*
>
> **NMC (2004)**

THINKING POINT

Mrs X aged 80 lives on her own and is normally independent, apart from having home help twice weekly. She suffers from mild dementia but has reasonable awareness of what is going on. She has one son, who visits weekly with his own family. She has been admitted to A & E following a fall and the x-rays confirmed a fractured neck of femur requiring surgery. The surgeons are concerned that on admission she is very confused and unable to understand relevant information or give informed consent.

1. What are the current guidelines for consenting individuals who lack mental capacity to consent?
2. If Mrs X has a 'living will' with advance directives, what would be the effect on her treatment?

LACK OF CAPACITY TO CONSENT AND BEST INTERESTS

Legal theory writers such as Hart (1968, p.5) recognize that informed consent is part of human freedom, but which nevertheless is not absolute as, 'there may be grounds justifying the legal coercion of the individual other than the prevention of harm to others'. UK law recognizes the clearly defined right of a patient not to be given treatment against his or her will, and not to be treated in the complete absence of consent. However, in interpretation of the law, judges in the UK have not developed a full doctrine of 'informed consent'. Lord Donaldson has subsequently set out the UK position as follows:

> *An adult patient who suffers from no mental incapacity has an absolute right to choose whether to consent to medical treatment, to refuse it, or to choose one rather than another of the treatments being offered ... This right of choice is not limited to decisions which others might regard as sensible. It exists notwithstanding that the reasons for making the choice are rational, irrational, unknown or even non-existent.*
>
> **Re T *[1992] 9 BMLR 46***

For patients who lack capacity there are new provisions in the Mental Capacity Act 2005 (Adults with Incapacity (Scotland) Act 2000). The advocate or 'deputy' is a person over the age of 18 who is appointed by the court. Under Section 20 of the Mental Capacity Act 2005, the deputy has limited powers and may not substitute the patient's decisions if they believe that the patient has the power to make that decision. For example, they may only decline treatment but may not demand treatment as doctors may treat a patient based on their own clinical judgements. Those who lack capacity are defined as follows:

> *(1) For the purposes of this Act, a person lacks capacity in relation to a matter if at the material time he is unable to make a decision for himself in relation to the matter because of an impairment of, or a disturbance in the functioning of, the mind or brain.*
>
> ***Section 2, Mental Capacity Act 2005***

To determine whether a patient has the necessary capacity, the test adopted is that in *Re C Test/Re C Advice: refusal of treatment* [1994] 1 WLR 290. At times it is possible that a patient's 'best interests' should be considered due to a patient's lack of capacity only after consideration of the following:

> *(3) He must consider (a) whether it is likely that the person will at some time have capacity in relation to the matter in question, and (b) if it appears likely that he will, when that is likely to be.*

> *(4) He must, so far as reasonably practicable, permit and encourage the person to participate, or to improve his ability to participate, as fully as possible in any act done for him and any decision affecting him.*
> ### Section 4, Mental Capacity Act 2005

In emergency situations, treatment may be given without seeking the patient's permission. The justification of such intervention is to preserve or save life. A doctor may not be prosecuted for trespass in emergency circumstances provided they can show that in so doing they were acting in the best interests of the patient. In situations dealing with those who lack mental capacity, either temporarily or permanently, decisions may also be made in the patient's best interests but there is a danger, prompting the need for clear guidelines. The best interests principle should take into account:

- *options for treatment or investigation which are clinically indicated;*
- *any evidence of the patient's previously expressed preferences, including an advance statement;*
- *your own and the health care team's knowledge of the patient's background, such as cultural, religious, or employment considerations;*
- *views about the patient's preferences given by a third party who may have other knowledge of the patient, for example the patient's partner, family, carer, tutor-dative (Scotland), or a person with parental responsibility;*
- *which option least restricts the patient's future choices, where more than one option (including non-treatment) seems reasonable in the patient's best interest.*
> ### General Medical Council (1998)

There are also exceptions under Article 5 (e) of HRA 1998 and public health laws for obtaining consent and for detention for people with an infectious disease, some cases of life-threatening situations and where a patient has previously clearly identified (in living wills) their wishes to decline treatment as illustrated in *Airedale N.H.S. Trust* v *Bland* [1993] A.C. 789:

> *It is established that the principle of self-determination requires that respect must be given to the wishes of the patient, so that if an adult patient of sound mind refuses, however unreasonably, to consent to treatment or care by which his life would or might be prolonged, the doctors responsible for his care must give effect to his wishes, even though they do not consider it to be in his best interests to do so.*
> ### per Lord Goff at p.864 C

In the event of an action for battery being brought against a clinician, their justification would also be that they acted through necessity. Necessity is a defence in an emergency situation (see below on capacity).

In the case of children, Section 1 of the Children Act 1989 which states (among other issues) the 'paramountcy' of the child's welfare is also applicable to the treatment of children as in 'the ascertainable wishes and feelings of the child (considered in the light of his age and understanding)' and 'any harm the child has suffered or is at risk of suffering'. (For more detailed information please see Chapter 4, Children's rights – the beginning of life to the age of majority.)

Gillick v *West Norfolk Area Health Authority* [1985] 3 All ER 492 is the authority for the principle that in certain circumstances a child under the age of 16 years could give valid consent (in this case contraceptives) without the involvement or knowledge of parents. The test was whether the child had a sufficient degree of understanding of what was proposed (Fraser formerly Gillick competence). This test is about capacity, not merely the ability to make a choice. However, in *Re S* [1994] 2 FLR 1065, a Scottish case, where a girl aged 15, who needed regular transfusions due to thalassaemia refused transfusion on religious grounds, it was held that she lacked the Fraser/Gillick competence due to her lack of understanding or full appreciation of the implication of not having a blood transfusion for a child under the age of 16. For children, however, parental consent cannot override a refusal of consent by a competent child who has the legal capacity to consent to his or her own treatment. The position is also clarified in Scots law, 'in the opinion of the qualified medical practitioner attending to him/her, he/she is capable of understanding the nature and the possible consequences of the procedure or treatment', under Section 2(4) of the Legal Capacity (Scotland) Act 1991.

Parents are normally expected by the law to make decisions on behalf of their children under the age of 18 in England or 16 in Scotland, unless the child has the capacity under 'Fraser competence'. Difficulties may arise for the nurse if there is conflict between the wishes of the parents and those of the child. Parents may not override a competent minor's decision. There is sometimes a need for a judicial review under the inherent 'parens patriae' or 'father of the country' (which is the jurisdiction of the court, which may be exercised by the High Court, Family Division) with the aim of making the child a ward of court. The role of the courts is highlighted in the following case. In *Re A (Children) Conjoined Twins: Surgical Separation* [2001] 2 WLR 480. Jodie and Mary were conjoined twins. Any separation would lead to saving Jodie's life (otherwise she would have died within six months) and the death of Mary (who would not have survived on her own). On religious grounds, the parents did not consent to an operation, which undoubtedly would have saved Jodie's life but led to the death of Mary. The Court of Appeal held that the operation should go ahead without the parents' consent.

In urgent cases, patients with mental health needs may be detained under Sections 2–5 of the Mental Health Act 1983 and be subject to compulsory treatment for the mental health condition under Section 63 of the Mental Health Act 1983. However *F* v *West Berkshire Health Authority and another (Mental Health Act Commission intervening)* [1989] 2 All ER at 545 shows that under Section 93(1) b of the same act, managing 'the affairs of patients' (limited to business affairs) did not extend to questions relating to the medical treatment of a patient. The court had therefore no jurisdiction to override such a patient's wishes on medical treatment. Part IV MHA 1983 (i.e. ss.56–64) applies only to medical treatment for mental disorder (i.e. psychiatric treatment).

Re R [1991]

R a 15-year-old girl refused antipsychotic treatment for mental illness, which was intermittent, with violent and suicidal symptoms. She seemed lucid and rational at the time of refusal. Held: by the High Court, that R was incompetent and could receive compulsory treatment though nevertheless only the court may override her refusal. Parents would have no right to make decisions on her behalf.

Section 47 of the National Assistance Act 1948 may be used in conjunction with the mental health compulsory admission powers, to remove a person from their usual place of abode to a place of safety, which could be for treatment.

THINKING POINT

Jim, a 31-year-old patient, who has been on treatment for bipolar illness for several years, is being detained under Section 4 of the Mental Health Act 1983, following a suicide attempt. He claims that he was being restrained and given injection medications against his will.

What are the ethical issues on informed consent to treatment if the above provision was not being followed?

RESEARCH AND CONSENT

The Nuremberg Code (1947) emerged as a result of the trial of that name officially called *United States* v *Karl Brandt*. The crimes committed were experiments with people who were subjected to inhuman treatment by the Nazi high command. An international agreement was put in place to regulate medical experiments and clinical trials. The code has ten requirements, among them:

> *1. The voluntary consent of the human subject is absolutely essential. This means that the person involved should have legal capacity to give consent: should be so situated as to be able to exercise free power of choice without the intervention of any element of force, fraud, deceit, duress, overreaching, or other ulterior form of constraint or coercion and should have sufficient knowledge and comprehension of the elements of the subject matter involved as to enable him to make an understanding and enlightened decision.*
>
> **Trials of War Criminals before the**
> **Nuremberg Military Tribunals 1946–49**

Research may involve clinical trials, which not only require consent but may also be regulated by contract law, where a participant is paid money in exchange for participation. Depending on the terms of agreement, the courts may not view favourably where there is an underlying contractual agreement. In the event of adverse reaction the defendant is entitled to a defence of 'volenti non fit injuria' (to a willing person, no injury is done). This means that any damages awarded for personal injury may be reduced substantially as a result. Others, however, see consent in research as, 'a convenient means of transferring responsibility for risk from the clinician or researcher to the informed' (Alderson and Goodey, 1998).

Sections 30–35 of the Mental Capacity Act 2005 now provide for advocacy in research, with additional safeguards (Section 33) for protection of any person lacking in consent who may be involved in research:

> *2) Nothing may be done to, or in relation to, him in the course of the research*
>
>   *(a) to which he appears to object (whether by showing signs of resistance or otherwise) except where what is being done is intended to protect him from harm or to reduce or prevent pain or discomfort, or*

(b) which would be contrary to
  (i) an advance decision of his which has effect, or
  (ii) any other form of statement made by him and not subsequently withdrawn, of which R is aware.
Section 33(2), Mental Capacity Act 2005

Following the Liverpool and Bristol Inquiry reports, the Health Service Circular HSC 2001/023 (Department of Health, 2001d, p.4) said a 'review of the law on the taking and use of human organs and tissue is currently in progress as part of the follow-up to the Liverpool and Bristol inquiry reports. Pending the outcome of this review, the model consent for treatment forms do not yet include a section on consent for the use of tissue removed during medical procedures, but the model policy makes clear that NHS organisations must have clear procedures in place to ensure that patients have the opportunity to refuse permission for such use if they wish'. As nurses are becoming more involved in research, they need to ensure that consent is properly obtained, especially if they are assisting others who may not have properly obtained this (RCN, 2005). Research involving human organs must always be in writing:

5) Consent in writing for the purposes of subsection (3) is only valid if –
  (a) it is signed by the person concerned in the presence of at least one witness who attests the signature,
  (b) it is signed at the direction of the person concerned, in his presence and in the presence of at least one witness who attests the signature, or
  (c) it is contained in a will of the person concerned made in accordance with the requirements of –
    (i) section 9 of the Wills Act 1837 (c. 26)
Human Tissue Act 2004

One important change introduced by the above statute into this area of law is that any such properly constituted consent may not be overruled by family members.

Another important area is highlighted in the scandals involving illegal organ storage and use for research. The Human Tissue Act (HTA) 2004 took effect on 1 September 2006, outlawing the following practices:

• the removal or storage of human tissue without prior consent;
• the taking and testing of DNA without consent;
• trafficking of organs.

The above offences now attract penalties ranging from a fine to three years' imprisonment or both.

The NHS Plan (2000) also gives further guidance on good practice and the need to obtain consent in research.

> **THINKING POINT**
>
> Consider the legal and ethical issues surrounding organ donation.

CONCLUSION

In practice, it is difficult for clinicians to determine whether a patient giving consent does so on the basis of a reasoned judgement, influence from others such as close family members, friends or other clinicians, or purely of their own accord. What is important is that unless it is an emergency, the patient should whenever possible be encouraged to make a choice having been afforded the opportunity to have sufficient information to help them to deliberate and make an important decision to consent to treatment or likewise, decline it. The difficulty arises when patients do not wish to have this information because of ignorance, fear of coming to terms with any outcome they may not wish to know (as far as risks of an operation are concerned) or they may believe that the nurse or doctor knows what is best for them. The role of the nurse should be to ensure that where possible, the patient's right to informed consent is guaranteed or at least the opportunity is afforded. With regard to treatment the ethics of self-determination and autonomy have since been recognized in common law:

> *It is established that the principle of self-determination requires that respect must be given to the wishes of the patient, so that, if an adult patient of sound mind refuses, however unreasonably, to consent to treatment or care by which his life would or might be prolonged, the doctors responsible for his care must give effect to his wishes, even ... though they do not consider it to be in his best interests to do so.*
>
> **Per Lord Goff in Airedale NHS Trust v Bland [1993] AC 789**

REFERENCES

Alderson P, Goodey C. Theories of consent. *BMJ* 1998; **317**: 1313–15.
Beauchamp TL, Childress JF. *Principles of biomedical ethics*, 5th edn. New York: Oxford University Press, 2001.

Blackburn S. *Being good: A short introduction to ethics*. Oxford: Oxford University Press, 2001.

Campbell A, Gillett G, Jones G. *Medical ethics*. Oxford: Oxford University Press, 2001.

Department of Health. *Guidance for clinicians: Model policy for consent to examination or treatment*, 2001a. www.dh.gov.uk/PolicyAndGuidance/HealthAndSocialCareTopics/Consent/ConsentGeneralInformation/fs/en, accessed 21/08/06.

Department of Health. *Good practice in consent: Achieving the NHS plan commitments to patient-centred practice*, HSC 2001/023, 2001b, www.dh.gov.uk.

Department of Health. *Good practice in consent implementation guide*. Crown Copyright, 2001c.

Department of Health. *Health Service Circular*, HSC 2001/023, 22 November 2001d, p.4.

Department of Health. NHS Plan, 2000, www.dh.gov.uk.

Doyal L. (2002) Good clinical practice and informed consent are inseparable. *Heart* 2002; **87**: 103–5, heart.bmj.com/cgi/content/abstract/87/2/103.

Fletcher L, Buka P. *A legal framework for caring: An introduction to law and ethics for healthcare professionals*. Basingstoke: Palgrave, 1999.

Furrow D. *Ethics: Key concepts in philosophy*. London: Continuum, 2005.

Giliken P, Bethwith S. *Tort*, 2nd edn. London: Sweet and Maxwell, 2004.

General Medical Council. Guidelines on seeking patients' consent: the ethical considerations, 1998. www.gmc-uk.org/guidance/current/library/consent.asp.

Hart HLA. *Punishment and responsibility*. Oxford: Oxford University Press, 1968.

Hoffman D, Rowe J. *Human rights in the UK: An introduction to the Human Rights Act 1998*. London: Pearson Longman, 2003.

Mental Health Act 1983 www.doh.gov.uk/mentalhealth/

Mill JS. *On Liberty; Everyman edition*. London: JM Dent, 1993.

Nursing and Midwifery Council. *Professional code of conduct and ethics: Standards for conduct, performance and ethics*, 2004.

Royal College of Nursing Research Society. *Informed consent in health and social care research*: RCN Guidance for Nurses, 2005.

Thompson I, Melia K, Boyd K. *Nursing ethics*. London: Churchill Livingstone, 2000.

Trials of War Criminals before the Nuremberg Military Tribunals under Control Council Law No. 10 Nuremberg October 1946–April 1949,

Washington. U.S. Government Printing Office (n.d.), vol. 2, pp. 181–2. www.cirp.org/library/ethics/nuremberg/

WHO. *Ethics of the Health Systems: Report of the Third Futures Forum for High-level Decision-makers*. Stockholm, Sweden 27–28 June 2002.

WHO (2003) www.euro.who.int/document/e77651.pdf

6 THE OLDER PERSON AND ABUSE

INTRODUCTION TO ABUSE

In different types of abusive situations, there is a common element – a breach of trust. The general principles are applicable to any type of abuse. This chapter focuses on the older patient although the principles are equally applicable to other groups of victims of abuse such as children and all other groups of vulnerable adults. Depending on the given situation, interventions to deal with the problem will be different. It is always difficult to establish the extent of abuse, due to possible underreporting as well as lack of evidence in support of any complaints as abuse may be perpetrated behind closed doors.

In contrast, in child abuse the Children Acts 1989 and 2004 have put in place effective measures to protect the child, although cases like that of Victoria Climbié (from children's perspective) have shown how ineffective the system can be if healthcare professionals fail to act proactively. In that area, the Children Act 1989 and the Children (Scotland) Act 1995 Regulations and Guidance, and the Children Act of 2004 were an appropriate response in providing safeguards such as a national children's champion who focuses on national issues related to child abuse. There is, however, no such specific provision for the protection of older people who may fall victim to abuse. When abuse involves the elderly, it could prove to be more difficult to manage if the abuser is a carer or a close family member, currently caring for the victim. Available responses are through piecemeal legislation without specific safeguards as in child law. This may cause confusion and frustration not only in the minds of the victims and their advocates but also in that of the perpetrator, who may not be aware that their action may be tantamount to abuse. An established definition of elder abuse is:

> *A single or repeated act or appropriate action occurring within a relationship where there is an expectation of trust which causes harm or distress to an older (dependent) person.*
>
> ***Action on Elder Abuse (1995)***

For the purposes of this chapter, the terms 'abuse' and 'elder abuse' are used interchangeably. The term 'elder abuse' has been in use for some time in the USA but is relatively new in the UK. (Bennett and Kingston (1995) are credited with adopting its use in the UK.) The debate on elder abuse has rekindled issues on the welfare and rights of people over the age of 65, especially those who may be dependent for their care and are therefore vulnerable and open to abuse. Abuse may take place either in the victim's own home or in an institution providing care.

Abuse involves violation of an individual's human and civil rights by any other person or persons covering a broad range of situations. This breach may be covered by law – the European Convention on Human Rights 1950 under Articles 3 and 17, Schedule 1 HRA 1998, although the number of cases which have gone to law in this area is limited.

Given the definition of abuse in the government paper Protection of Vulnerable Adults (POVA) it is possible to conceive of victims of elder abuse as only those who are dependent on another for their care (POVA, 2000). In fact any older person may be subject to abuse without the 'dependency' requirement. The emphasis should therefore be on 'vulnerability' instead. Studies have shown that 40 per cent of members who are practising district nurses have either witnessed or been aware of elder abuse, with half of them having knowledge of a patient who had been a victim of abuse (Community and District Nursing Association (CDNA), 2004).

CLASSIFICATION OF ABUSE

A survey of older people (Bennett, 2002) suggested that the only three broad areas they (as potential and actual victims) considered to amount to abuse were as follows:

- Neglect – this may be caused by the victim themselves or may be a result of omissions of others.

- Violation of human rights which may have legal as well as medical implications.
- Deprivation of some privilege, which may include substitution of choices and decisions.

The above categories demonstrate that there are aspects of abuse that elderly people themselves may not consider to be abuse. Therefore they may not feel it necessary to report the abuse and may consider it as their 'lot', an acceptable phenomenon (Bennett, 2002). Understanding classifications of abuse is important for healthcare professionals, so that they may appreciate the range of issues they may have to deal with. It is generally accepted that there are at least five types of abuse.

There is a consensus of other common classifications, which includes the following:

- Physical: this involves contact or battery, which may include inflicting physical harm such as restraining as well as the inappropriate administration of medications.
- Psychological: this would include swearing, threats of violence, insults, mental torture, humiliation, belittling someone and social isolation.
- Financial/property: this covers misappropriation of all forms of possessions belonging to an elderly person (see Chapter 7, Diversity and equality – anti-discriminatory practice). This would also include unauthorized and unexplained changes in wills and suspect bank or benefit transactions, often with the alleged abuser as beneficiary.
- Sexual: this involves rape, indecent assault, as well as any form of unwarranted touch and sexual innuendo (which is strictly speaking 'psychological'). Any sexual activity must be between consenting adults with mental capacity.
- Neglect: this may be carried out by others such as family members or carers, or self-inflicted. In some cases, the victim may not be aware of the resulting harm. It is nevertheless possible that self-neglect can take place, hence the need for a thorough investigation before accusing carers or family members. Should a person choose to take their own life, it is no longer a criminal offence for individuals to take their own life, under Section 2 of the Suicide Act 1961. As well as a breach of duty of care, professionals may be found to be in breach of their duty of care when they fail to act to prevent abuse.

These categories are based on the British Geriatrics Society Classification (1998). The Department of Health (2000) added another category 'discriminatory abuse' to this list. The government White Paper, No Secrets (2000), introduced a further category, that of discriminatory abuse (sometimes described as 'institutional'). This considers abuse as a result of inadequate provisions for the elderly – it is questionable whether this should be a separate class (of ageism) from other grounds of discrimination such as religion, race, gender and sexual orientation (which may be recognized by the law). There is now a provision in law under the Employment Equality (Age) Regulations 2006.

An abuser could potentially be 'from a wide range of people including relatives and family members, as well as professional staff, paid care workers, volunteers, other service users, neighbours, friends and associates, people who deliberately exploit vulnerable people and strangers' (paragraph 2.10 No Secrets, Department of Health, 2000).

It is important to consider the effectiveness of current responses in light of any staff training as well as clear guidelines, which should be proactive to minimize the risk of and counter abuse. However, these do not always offer sufficient protection to a victim. Abuse involving violent acts may amount to a criminal offence provided the elements of a crime, a guilty intention (*mens rea*) and a guilty act (*actus reus*) are proven. The Crown Prosecution Service under criminal law may prosecute the perpetrator. The difficulty is that the generic category of domestic abuse ranges from seemingly minor and harmless actions such as psychological abuse or harassment to those with more serious consequences like rape, serious assault or murder. It is possible that there may be 'window dressing' of the criminal act by using the term 'abuse' instead of more serious terminology. The difference between violence in general and elder abuse is the context within which it generally takes place. Research based on the British Crime Survey (1995) suggests that the highest number of assaults took place in the home, with '8 out of 10' victims of abuse being women (Donnellan, 2001, p.2). Following several hospital episodes, signs of suspected abuse may be 'discovered' by a healthcare professional on admission assessments in Accident and Emergency Departments, often unrelated to the apparent reason for admission:

> *The signs of abuse are not always very obvious and may be uncovered secondary to other issues, perhaps when a client is admitted to care following alleged 'falls', clinical findings may not be consistent with the pre-admission history and the client's health status.*
>
> **Fletcher and Buka (1999, p.155)**

The central problem facing the healthcare professional in dealing with vulnerable adult abuse is that it is difficult to prove abuse and a victim may not wish to report it if this involves a close family member. Nevertheless, if they suspect abuse healthcare professionals are duty bound to report it to other members of the multidisciplinary team. They must follow their own local guidelines on the process for reporting abuse. Nurses may find themselves in a dilemma between the need for confidentiality, the necessity to breach this if their patient's safety is under threat (if a crime has been or is about to be committed), if disclosure is in the public interest, as required by statute or if ordered to disclose by a court of law.

> *5.2 You should seek patients' and clients' wishes regarding sharing information with their family and others. When a patient is considered incapable of giving permission you should consult relevant colleagues.*
>
> **NMC Code of Professional Conduct (2004)**

The Caldicott principles provide further clarification in this area (Department of Health, 1997). Any disclosure of confidential information is subject to the Data Protection Act 1998.

THEORIES OF ABUSE

Criminological theories attempt to offer some explanations on why perpetrators become violent and abusive and why some victims accept abuse as part and parcel of life. There is a link between the term 'abuse' and its generic term 'violence'. The difference is that violence may take place between strangers while abuse occurs within a trusting relationship between the abuser and the victim. In the latter situation there is a breach of trust and there may be fear and dependency from the victim's perspective. Often, deception is involved but it is unlikely that there is collusion on the part of the victim. Usually there is no choice in the outcome from the view of the victim as they may have been let down by those they trusted. A further element is the imbalance of power between the abuser and the victim. This is the position in which older people who are vulnerable find themselves. Only the main theories are included here in the attempt to explain why violence is perpetrated, with vulnerable people in general as well as the elderly in particular, at the receiving end.

Biological and psychological theories

These two terms are related and have been put forward to explain how biological or psychological make-up may affect the behaviour of a potential abuser. The main theories aim to link behaviour with genetic traits, which are thought to cause a predisposition towards violent behaviour. It has been suggested that some violent men possess an extra male 'Y' male chromosome (Herrnstein and Murray, 1994). For some individuals this may include paranoia, which is supposedly determined by abnormalities in the chromosomes relating to the XXY and the XYY factors (Williams, 2001). This condition is treatable through hormonal therapy. From the above, there has been a suggestion of a link to criminality for the XYY factor, which is the syndrome where the extra male chromosome is present and, another view is 'that chromosome abnormality and criminality are not closely related, and more significantly, if general explanations are wanted, the incidence of XXY and XYY males is so rare as to be of little practical significance' (Williams, 2001, p.147).

The so-called 'naturalistic studies' have suggested that the children of criminals are more likely to become criminals themselves in later life, as a 'natural tendency' (Fitzgerald *et al.*, 1981, p.371). Eysenck (1977) however has explained this behaviour as merely conditioned responses, which are achieved through operant conditioning, in the Pavlovian sense.

Cultural and social learning theories

These theories attribute the apparently higher level of domestic violence and abuse of wives and children in some cultures than in others to a learned process of the adoption of certain norms of behaviour from an early age. Some authorities put forward the view that 'in a homogeneous society, these (norms) were enacted into laws and upheld by the members of that society because they accepted them as right' (Sellin cited by Williams, 2001, p.439). The values of a society in how it relates to the treatment of women seem to be based on the acceptance of certain norms of behaviour. The cultural basis of the prevalence of violence only serves to explain the existence of accepted standards of behaviour in any given situation. This does not necessarily lend support to the myth that some ethnic groups are more violent than others towards their female partners. Some studies have shown that cultural behaviour is passed on from generation to generation. On people in relationships, Hertzberger (1996, p.109) concluded that the 'majority of abusive spouses and their victims are more likely to have a history of abuse by their parents'. These norms are supposed to reinforce the concept of a male-dominated society, with women, children and the elderly as victims, and this is unfortunate as it may give the impression that most abusers are male. It is not possible to prove conclusively that culture, whether racial, geographical or social class related, is per se responsible for domestic violence and the abuse of vulnerable people such as the elderly. It is possible that partner abuse may be used as a tool to exercise control and subjugate the weaker person. Other attempts to explain violence in the family context have been based on social learning. Some base domestic violence and cultural abuse on the 'subculture of violence', by attributing it to men's 'susceptibility', which Curtis (1975) put down to racism and economic oppression.

The social learning theory of Albert Bandura (1977) is one of the most fascinating contributions from behaviourists who have made an important contribution to the debate on learned criminal behaviour which is said to result in abuse of elderly persons by their own children, if the latter have been brought up previously experiencing a culture of abuse. The basis of this theory is that behaviour is learnt through observation of violent behaviour. This could be explained by a negative effect not only from the family, but also from society as a whole (which may be seen as uncaring towards its older persons) as well as media sources such as television and press, 'children and adults acquire attitudes, emotional responses and new styles of conduct through filmed television modelling' (Bandura, 1997, p.39). This process is called 'modelling'. This would explain the future presence of criminal or violence behaviour in individuals who have been exposed to violence as children. As to the question why there are more men abusers and more female victims, Bandura (1973) suggests that 'boys more readily imitate the aggression they observe in others ... girls in contrast refrain from imitating, unless explicitly informed that aggressive behaviour is acceptable' (cited in Hertzberger, 1996, p.118).

Other factors, for example alcohol and drug abuse, can be contributory to violence and elder abuse, and may sometimes be used as an excuse. Studies have shown a correlation between alcohol and substances and criminal behaviour in the home by someone who already has a criminal propensity (Williams, 2001). Alcohol is not only a depressant but may remove inhibitions, thus making it easier for a carer of an elderly person who has experienced pent-up feelings of stress to be more aggressive and abusive. It is possible that alcohol will be used as an excuse for violence. There may very well be other related causes, such as 'paying back' old scores to a previously abusive parent or spouse for whose care they may be responsible.

The feminist perspective – learned helplessness

Feminist theories generally attribute the trend towards violence as evidence of the inequality between men and women. This view is consistent with other factors such as economic dependence and the lower earning power of women, as well as a conflict of interests between spouses. These principles could apply to any relationships or equally to men who are subjected to abuse in their own homes by women. Some attribute the 'imbalance' between men and women to men's 'economic strength' and support in the home (Williams, 2001, p.327). The issue of dependence can limit the victim in the options available to them.

> *I remember the first time he hit me, he was quite sorry and I forgave him because I was madly in love with him and I thought, oh hell it was just one of those things and it wouldn't happen again, so I suppose the first time he did it he got away with it, but it just got worse and worse.*
>
> ### National Children's Home (1994, p.22)

The sense of 'helplessness', according to Walker's model, is where the victim becomes dependent and loses their self-confidence as they may feel completely controlled by the perpetrator. The suggested 'cycle of violence' (Walker, 2002, p.1) has the same subsequent ongoing pattern once it starts. First, the tension starts to build. This is followed by actual violence consisting of psychological abuse and then possibly battering incidents. This behaviour may be calculated and explosive and usually results in violent confrontation. As soon as the violent episode has ended the perpetrator apparently becomes contrite and apologizes for his behaviour and may even shower the victim with gifts and romanticism. The cycle may actually get worse over time. The importance of such theories is that they aim to explain human behaviour from both the perpetrator's point of view and the victim's reaction to abuse.

INTERVENTIONS IN GENERAL

Before responding vigorously to allegations or apparent elder abuse, it may not in the first instance be necessary to warrant legal or other formal interventions, as things may not be what they seem. There may also be a danger of intervening informally or reporting the matter to authorities in that a victim may through their own choice be held responsible for their own self-neglect. It is important for clear guidelines in the clinical environment to minimize the risk to vulnerable older people. Doing nothing in the hope that things will resolve themselves is not an option as it is not hard to imagine the outcome of doing nothing. The problem is that without the active cooperation of a victim in any complaint investigation where there is suspected abuse, it may be difficult if not impossible to prosecute (Potter, 2004). Interventions should always be through interdisciplinary settings so as to encourage a balanced and fairer outcome for both the patient and the alleged abuser, especially if this turns out to be unsubstantiated. Those involved should include multidisciplinary healthcare professionals, as well as other inter-agency groups such as social services, the police and any local advocacy agencies (for example Victim Support and Citizens Advice Bureau) to provide support. Cases of suspected abuse in which there is evidence of a criminal act or involving serious injury or death should always be reported to the police. Thereafter the Crown Prosecution Service may decide to prosecute on the basis of the evidence, or may not prosecute if it is not in the public interest to do so. Healthcare professionals may be reluctant to report the matter if there is any doubt, as they may be concerned about making the situation worse for the victim should their suspicions turn out to be ill founded. Abuse may amount to a criminal offence if the guilty intention is proven. Unintentional abuse also has adverse effects on an elderly victim, and depending on the degree of recklessness, if proven, could also be criminal negligence. Following several cases of elder abuse that have come to light, the government has responded with its White Paper, No Secrets: the Protection of Vulnerable Adults (POVA, 2000).

Case study

Fitzgerald (the director of Action on Elder Abuse) pointed out that many people would be familiar with the case of Victoria Climbié ... but few knew about Margaret Panting, a 78-year-old woman from Sheffield who died after suffering 'unbelievable cruelty' while living with relatives. After her death in 2001, a post-mortem found 49 injuries on her body including cuts probably made by a razor blade and cigarette burns. She had moved from sheltered accommodation to her son-in-law's home – five weeks later she was dead but as the cause of Margaret Panting's death could not be established, no one was ever charged. An inquest in 2002 recorded an open verdict.

House of Commons (2004)

The link between crime rates and elder abuse is not always easy to establish. An overview of related crime rates demonstrates that certain abuse-type crimes may also be on the increase (Home Office, 2003). Victim gender differences may also be indicative of the extent of the vulnerability of older people. Up to 20% of persons over 85 years old attending A&E presented with trauma conditions, which could be linked to abuse (British

Geriatrics Society, 1998). These figures should however be treated with caution as they do not distinguish between other violent crimes and abuse (Home Office, 2003).

THINKING POINT

M and S are the married daughters of Jim X who was now unable to cope on his own and required to be placed in a local authority nursing home three months following his wife's death (he had been the main carer for several years). Over the last two months they have noticed that he appears to be losing a lot of weight and he has bruises on his upper arms. He is very sleepy whenever they visit; the staff nurse in charge says that he has been given (as required) nitrazepam tablets as he keeps other residents awake. This makes him rather groggy and unsteady during the day. They also noticed that he often smells of urine, has not been bathed for several days and they often have to ask the staff to change him as it seems to take a long time before he is changed, during the duration of their visits. They (staff) say that the reason he is not attended to is that he refuses to get changed. He also appears to be frightened of one particular male agency carer. He begs his daughters to take him home.

They suspect abuse. Consider the case in the light of your local guidelines for managing elder abuse.

CRIMINAL LAW RESPONSES

Where there is evidence of a criminal act having taken place, the matter should be reported to the police. Based on the investigation and evidence, the Crown Prosecution Service may subsequently prosecute the abuser. It is necessary to prove the *mens rea* (a guilty mind) and *actus reus* (a guilty act). The burden of proof depends on the 'preponderance' or persuasiveness of evidence or how convincing the evidence may be, and this should go beyond reasonable doubt. An example is when there is a history of unexplained falls as well as suspicious behaviour. Some of the areas of law concerned with abuse are:

- Trespass to the person offences are covered by the Offences against the Person Act 1861, involving ranges of physical contact resulting in harm. In England, assault consists of verbal abuse only while battery is contact ranging from unwanted physical touch to inflicting actual harm while in Scotland assault covers both aspects. Unwanted treatment, for instance giving a patient an unwanted enema while purportedly acting 'in their best interests', is one example of the offence of battery. The patient's right to privacy under Article 8 of the HRA 1998 is applicable.

- Property offences are subject to Sections 1 and 15 of the Theft Act 1968, the Theft Act 1978 and the Theft (Amendment) Act 1996. This may involve a criminal offence of openly stealing goods (Section 1) or the more subtle aspect of obtaining goods by deception (Section 15). For theft offences, please see Chapter 8, Theft, fraud and deception – patient property.
- Sexual offences are mainly covered by the Sexual Offences Act 1984 and the Sexual Offences (Amendment) Act 2003. The courts will take the view that in cases where consent is given by a patient who lacks capacity, that is not valid, hence an absolute offence where children are involved.
- Exclusion orders were introduced into s 40A of the Powers of Criminal Courts (Sentencing) Act 2000, by Section 46 of The Criminal Justice and Courts Services Act 2000. This enables the courts to ban a perpetrator from entering the premises (where the elder abuse victim is currently living) for a period of up to two years.
- Anti-social behaviour orders (ASBOs) came into being under the Crime and Disorder Act 1998. Subject to Section 1 (a), an offender whose behaviour harasses or causes 'alarm or distress' may be excluded (under a court order) from the alleged victim's place of residence. The landlord, the police or local authority may apply for this for protection of the victim.

CIVIL REMEDIES

In addition, a victim can also seek remedies in the civil courts for personal injury, in conjunction with the above (criminal) measures. The victim may apply for an injunction (which is a court order preventing conduct such as contact with the victim). Breach of such a court order will result in penalties. The following categories demonstrate the nature and levels of current legal responses.

Personal injury claims

It is a long-established principle in negligence under tort law, that if an individual, who is owed a duty of care, suffers harm as a result of another's negligence they are entitled to damages for personal injury. The basic duty of care originated in *Donoghue* v *Stevenson* [1932] and is developed in *Caparo Industries* v *Dickman* [1990] below. Carers owe a duty of care not to harm the persons they provide care to through their actions or omissions. If the nurse as a carer has been in breach of a duty of care and the victim suffers harm (personal injury) as a result, the victim may be entitled to recover damages in compensation under tort law (or law of delict in Scotland).

In his famous judgement, in the same case, Lord Atkins established the duty of care principle; that:

> You must take reasonable care to avoid acts or omissions which you can reasonably foresee would be likely to injure your neighbour. Who, then, in law is my neighbour? The answer seems to be – persons who are so closely and directly affected by my act that I ought reasonably to have them in contemplation as being so affected when I am directing my mind to the acts or omissions which are called in question.
>
> **Lord Atkins at p.562 Donoghue v Stevenson [1932] AC 562**

A three-stage test for determining 'duty of care' has subsequently been applied by the courts in establishing the duty of care in the following case.

Caparo v Dickman [1990] 2AC 605

This was a landmark case where an auditor working for the defendants had compiled a report for Caparo, which showed that Fidelity Co was in profit. Relying on this information Caparo bought shares. As it turned out this was not the case and the plaintiff's shareholders lost money. The shareholders for Caparo sued the auditors who had compiled the report for negligence. It was held that there was no sufficient proximity of relationship between auditors and shareholders, thus setting out the three-stage test for duty of care:

- Whether there was foreseeability of harm?
- Whether there was a sufficient proximity of relationship between the parties?
- Whether it was just, fair and equitable for the court to impose a duty of care?

Section 46 of the Domestic Violence, Crime and Victims Act 2004 introduced a provision for the court to issue non-molestation orders for the protection of victims of abuse, provided the victim is living in the same household as the perpetrator of the abuse. There is law for protecting occupancy rights in Scotland in the form of the Matrimonial Homes (Family Protection) (Scotland) Act 1981. Such legislation may nevertheless still be breached, thus putting the victim of abuse at an even greater risk of retribution.

PUBLIC AUTHORITIES AND HUMAN RIGHTS

The European Convention on Human Rights 1950 became part of UK human rights law after the passing of the HRA 1998 (implemented in 2000).

Under articles in Schedule 1, for example Articles 3 and 17, a victim of abuse may take a public body such as a local authority or a healthcare trust to court. In dealing with them, the issue of abuse may not be resolved in the UK courts and then an appeal is lodged to the European Court of Human Rights in Strasbourg. It also means that a victim may rely on the human rights legislation (in UK courts) without going to Strasbourg.

Although this was intended to enhance the rights of victims, the statute does not go far enough as it is limited to abuse in a caring environment which is provided by a public body only. A victim of abuse who is in care provided by a private home may not rely on this legislation but instead pursue criminal and civil law.

OLDER VICTIMS WITH MENTAL HEALTH NEEDS

It may be necessary to protect an elderly patient with mental health needs. In this case, compulsory orders are available for compulsory admission to a healthcare facility for either a victim of abuse or the perpetrator (who has mental health needs) (Sections 2–5, Mental Health Act 1983 or corresponding aspects of the Mental Health (Scotland) Act 1984). The mental health provisions may be used to protect the needs of individuals with mental health needs or those of their carers. For example, under Section 37 of the Mental Heath Act 1983, the courts have powers to order hospital admission or guardianship. Alternatively, Section 43 of the same act defines the power of magistrates' courts to commit for restriction order. The Mental Capacity Act 2005 also provides additional protection for a vulnerable person to appoint another person to look after their interests regarding consent to treatment, as they may be open to abuse. Mental capacity for the purposes of this statute includes both those who may have a temporary or permanent need. This power includes treatment as well as financial interests.

INTER-AGENCY WORKING AND ABUSE

For nurses Paragraph 3 of the Nursing and Midwifery Council (2004) code of professional conduct requires the client's informed consent to treatment (treatment here is used in its widest context). Paragraph 8, NMC (2004) code of professional conduct requires the nurse to 'identify' and minimize any risk to patients and clients. The essential elements should include evaluation and assessment on the presence or absence of informed consent. This may be due to temporary or permanent causes. This is important because of the dependency and the imbalance of power within the client–carer relationship. The healthcare professional should be aware of the ethical values underpinning respect for their patient's values and ensure their right to autonomy or informed choice. Failure to consider this right may result in breach of human rights.

The government's response to several cases of abuse in the press was to produce some guidance in the form of the White Paper, Modernizing Social Services – No Secrets, reinventing the definition of a vulnerable adult as someone, 'who may be in need of community care services by reason of mental or other disability, age, or illness; and who is or may be unable to take care of him or herself against significant harm or exploitation' (Department of Health, 2000, paragraph 2.3), but as discussed above, this is not enough. The White Paper is seriously flawed as it does not include those who may be victims of abuse but who do not receive community services (Parliamentary Select Committee on Health, February 2004). The aim of the above guidance is to bring together the various agencies responsible for the provision of care in the development of policies and procedures for the protection of vulnerable adults (including the elderly) from abuse. Health and social care providers benefit from working with all other agencies that may be involved in the care of the client.

THINKING POINT

Mrs X is an 84-year-old lady who has been widowed for 10 years, having had no children in her marriage. She has a niece who lives in South Africa who never visits and she last saw her at her husband's funeral. Apart from that time, they never keep in touch. Mrs X has become increasingly dependent on private carers as well as on her neighbours Peter and his wife. He happens to be a qualified practising psychiatric nurse and his wife is a district healthcare assistant. They pop in every day and help with the shopping. Over the years Peter and his wife have become very close to Mrs X who often treats them like family. She buys them and the children gifts for Christmas and birthdays. Peter also pays her bills and is an authorized signatory to Mrs X's bank accounts. She has three accounts but does not keep track of the large amounts in the bank since her husband died. She trusts Peter with her debit cards and the district nurse who visits regularly suspects he might be withdrawing unauthorized large sums of money without Mrs X's knowledge. Peter has just bought himself a car paid for with Mrs X's money but when confronted by the district nurse he says he needs the car for taking Mrs X to the hospital for her appointments, even though he uses the car for personal use.

Consider what actions you would need to take in order to protect the patient.

The problem is that it is difficult to monitor what happens in individual private homes where most abuse is alleged to take place (CDNA, 2004). In cases which may be drawn to their attention, social workers have at their disposal the powerful protective powers of Section 47 of the National Assistance Act 1948, to help them to remove a victim of abuse to a place of safety if it is felt that they may be a danger to themselves or to others. In practice, this is difficult to enforce unless the victim has mental health needs. The Mental Capacity Act 2005 introduced additional guarantees of health-care advocacy from April 2007, bringing English law into line with Scottish law, Mental Health (Care and Treatment) (Scotland) Act 2003. Informal arrangements alone may occasionally be adequate when the patient, family members or friends all agree that the multidisciplinary team can pre-empt the situation by putting in place measures to minimize harm or remove a victim from the abusive environment. The following statute provides a wel-come relief for a carer who may require respite and thus proved some relief.

> *The carer may request the local authority, before they make their decision as to whether the needs of the relevant person call for the provision of any services, to carry out an assessment of his ability to provide and to continue to provide care for the relevant person.*
> **Section 1(b) Carers (Recognition and Services) Act 1995**

CONCLUSION

Scotland has provided personal care, something which may be important in lessening the chances of abuse in the home (Community Care and Health (Scotland) Act 2002). Addressing elder abuse should be inclusive and con-sider the carers who may themselves be vulnerable elders, 'many care givers express feelings of frustration, despair, and worry of not being cared for themselves, they often feel the situation is beyond their control' (Bradley, 1996, p.1).

The introduction of the Public Interest Disclosure Act 1998 makes it easier for healthcare workers who 'blow the whistle' on suspected abuse to be protected against victimization. In practice, victims may still be reluctant to go through the difficult procedure of having to give evidence against a loved one or losing them through imprisonment or enforced separation for their own protection. This was recognized by the House of Commons (2004, paragraph 2), in the Government's response to the recommendations and conclusions of the Health Select Committee's Inquiry into Elder Abuse. It is clear that as long as the causes for violent crimes exist, it is possible that vulnerable patients may be victims. Elder abuse tends to be subtle and secretive, and vulnerable older people may continue to suffer in secret. The importance of the healthcare professional's intervention is in being able to recognize the signs, being proactive and in being able to prevent abuse from occurring.

REFERENCES

Action on Elder Abuse (AEA). Bulletin, May–June, 1995.

Bandura A. *Social learning theory*. New York: General Learning Press, 1977.

Bandura A. *Social learning theory*. London: Prentice Hall, 1997.

Bandura A, Ribes-Inesta E. *Analysis of delinquency and aggression*. New York: Lawrence Erlbaum Associates, 1976.

Bennett G. Age and ageing, British Geriatric Society, 2002, www.bgs.org.uk/Publications/age_ageing.htm.

Bennett G, Kingston P. *Concepts, theories and interventions*. London: Chapman & Hall, 1995.

Bradley M. Caring for older people: Elder abuse. *BMJ* 1996; **313**: 548–50.

British Geriatrics Society (BGS). The abuse of older people, 1998. www.bgs.org.uk/accessed 29/12/06.

Community and District Nursing Association (CDNA). Elder abuse, 2004, www.cdna.tvu.ac.uk.

Community and District Nursing Association (CDNA). (2004) http://www.thecampaigncompany.co.uk/cdna/.

Curtis L. *Violence, race and culture*. Lexington, MA: Lexington Books, 1975.

Department of Health. No secrets, guidance on developing and implementing multi-agency policies and procedures to protect vulnerable adults from abuse, HSC 2001/007: LAC (2001)12, Crown Copyright, London, 2000.

Department of Health. Caldicott Guardians, HSC 1999/012, 1997.

Donnellan C. *Alcohol abuse issues*. Cambridge: Independence Educational Publishers, 2001.

Eysenck H. *Crime and personality*, 3rd edition. London: Routledge and Kegan Paul, 1977.

Fitzgerald M, McLennan G, Pawson J. *Crime and society: readings in history and theory*. London: Open University Press, 1981.

Fletcher L, Buka P. *A legal framework for caring*. Basingstoke: Palgrave Macmillan, 1999.

Herrnstein RJ, Murray C. *The bell curve: the reshaping of American life by differences in intelligence*. Free Press: New York, 1994.

Hertzberger S. *Violence within the family*. Sociology perspectives, Oxford Social Psychology Series. Boulder, CO: Westview Press, 1996.

HPO. What major theories explain the cause of men's violence against women? 2003, www.hs-scgcca/hppb/family accessed on 24/12/03.

Home Office. Crime in England and Wales, London: Home Office Statistical Bulletin, Crown Copyright, 2003, http://www.helptheaged.org.uk/CampaignsNews/News/_items/elderabusecasestudies.htm, accessed 02/02/05.

House of Commons. The Government's response to the recommendations and conclusions of the Health Select Committee, Crown Copyright, 2004.

NCH. The hidden victims: Children and domestic violence. London, NCH for Children, 1994, http://www.nch.org.uk/information/index.

Nursing and Midwifery Council. *Professional code of conduct and ethics*. London: NMC, 2004.

Potter J. (2004) Behind closed doors: Abuse of the elderly patient. *Nursing in Practice* 2004; **14**: 21–3.

Walker L. The cycle of violence: Lenore Walker's model. 2002, http://mesa6.mesastate.edu.

Williams K. *The Oxford handbook of criminology*. Oxford: Oxford University Press, 2001.

7 DIVERSITY AND EQUALITY: ANTI-DISCRIMINATORY PRACTICE

INTRODUCTION AND BACKGROUND TO DISCRIMINATION

This chapter considers the importance of the ethical principle in the need to provide care for all patients, with diversity in mind, fairly and without preferential treatment. Owing to the complexity of this area, which affects patient's rights, the chapter aims to give an overview of aspects of discrimination. This is not always clear-cut, as any patient's treatment will be dependent on their needs and on the basis of defining what those needs are. To those receiving care, certain practices may be seen as discrimination. Any patient's needs are those which contribute to good health, as stated in the WHO Constitution:

> *The enjoyment of the highest attainable standard of health is one of the fundamental rights of every human being without distinction of race, religion, political belief, economic or social condition.*
> **WHO Constitution (1946)**

It is also clear that while some patients are aware of and are able to assert their right not to be discriminated against, many may not be prepared to complain or may simply lack the knowledge and ability to do so. Where discrimination is established there may not only be breach of an ethical principle but also legal consequences and/or implications for professional registration.

Most of the anti-discrimination case law is based on employment law; nevertheless, the principles therein are also applicable to healthcare law where a patient feels discriminated against. Anti-discriminatory practice is required by law, for example the Race Relations Act 1976.

Sometimes individuals may have deeply rooted, stereotyped attitudes prejudicial towards a certain group of people. Prejudice has long been defined as

Hostile or negative attitudes based on ignorance and faulty or incomplete knowledge. It is characterized by a tendency to assign identical characteristics to whole groups regardless of individual variations.
Twitchin and Demuth (1985, p.170)

At the end of the Second World War, it was recognized internationally that something needed to be done to ensure fair treatment of individuals and this extends to healthcare provision. Under the auspices of the United Nations, the Universal Declaration of Human Rights (1948) emerged, recognizing, inter alia, that:

Article 2: Everyone is entitled to all the rights and freedoms set forth in this Declaration, without distinction of any kind, such as race, colour, sex, language, religion, political or other opinion, national or social origin, property, birth or other status. Furthermore, no distinction shall be made on the basis of the political, jurisdictional or international status of the country or territory to which a person belongs, whether it is independent, trust, non-self-governing or under any other limitation of sovereignty.
United Nations (1948)

If ethical principles are followed, this means that the nurse must balance patients' interests according to their needs as well as subject to available resources.

DISCRIMINATION IN HEALTHCARE PROVISION AND ETHICAL VALUES

Clearly, not all grounds of discrimination are recognized by and enforceable under existing law. One example is discrimination on the grounds of social status or class. This may often be subtle and difficult to prove. It can nevertheless be argued that the Code of Professional Conduct and Ethics (NMC, 2004) requires the provision of non-discriminatory practice by nurses.

The concept of 'discrimination' is difficult to define especially as it is widely used with a variety of slightly differing contexts.

THINKING POINT

Ms C, a high court judge (she has a history of complaining and threatening nurses with legal action), comes in as a private patient on an acute NHS medical ward and appears to be given better treatment in comparison to other patients. On this occasion, she will be moved into a side room; this is not based on clinical need but merely to keep her quiet. Mr J, a recovering alcoholic man in his late seventies admitted with other medical problems had been put in the side room due to being noisy at night-time. He is then moved out of this side room. The other patients in the bay where he is to be moved to are not happy.
What action would you recommend?

This type of situation is placed within the requirement for 'fairness' in ethics (Beauchamp and Childress, 2001). For a nurse responsible for patient care to respond to the needs of patients from 'diverse' backgrounds effectively, they need to avoid favouritism or disadvantaging individual patients. Providing preferential treatment for one patient happens to detract from other patients' rights while also compromising the treatment of other 'less advantaged' patients. This may mean that the care given to the latter then falls below the expected standards of a person possessing their skills under the Bolam principle (see the case of *Bolam* v *Friern Hospital Committee* [1957] 2 All ER 118. All professional codes of conduct for healthcare personnel require of their members fair treatment as well as non-discrimination of patients or clients.

The Human Rights Act 1998 came into force in 2000. It was felt however that the issue of discrimination was fragmented and this culminated in a major change with the enactment of the Equality Act (EA) 2006. The catalyst for change was the House of Commons itself in a body which would police the implementation on human rights and related anti-discriminatory legislation, 'an independent commission would be the most effective way of achieving the shared aim of bringing about a culture of respect for human rights' (Joint Committee on Human Rights, 2002–03).

The EA 2006 statute now brings together existing legislation by updating legislation in most of the six areas of discrimination legislation. This was also meant to be some kind of legal 'umbrella', which aimed to bring together all types of discrimination. Most of the existing anti-discrimination legislation remains intact and this statute aims to coordinate the fight against discrimination by having one central body, the commission. The importance of this area of legislation is that victims should feel that they have access to justice and are not put off by any red tape. The effectiveness of anti-discriminatory legislation depends on the willingness of victims to complain. The difficulty is that while some persons on the receiving end may wish to complain about discrimination, others who lack the competence, such as incapacitated patients or those who lack knowledge about their rights, may do nothing. Some patients may feel that they do not wish to 'rock the boat' and indeed choose to put up with discrimination in the case of victimization.

COMMON GROUNDS FOR DISCRIMINATION RECOGNIZED BY THE LAW

Discrimination goes to the heart of patients' fundamental human rights, which must be respected as 'all men *and women* (emphasis added) are created equal and independent … they derive rights inherent and inalienable, among which are the preservation of life and liberty and the pursuit of happiness' (Thomas Jefferson cited in Boyd, 1950, p.423).

All types of discrimination involve breach of these fundamental rights through mistreatment or treatment of one person less favourably in comparison to another, as well as the positive aspect where the favoured individual is given privileged or preferential treatment, again, in comparison to others. There is also the negative side where the victim of discrimination is treated less favourably than their counterparts. Both aspects are equally unacceptable in nursing as they result in unfair and unequal provision of care, hence the reason why discrimination should be tackled as an infringement of patients' rights as much as that of any other ordinary citizens.

The converse or negative aspect, which means that one or more patients are given preferential treatment, should also be considered, even if this means that this may be difficult to prove. The effect on the disadvantaged person(s) is the same, being left out in the cold. The victim(s) may therefore have grounds for discrimination under the law. This is clearly in breach of ethical principles (which are embraced by the Beauchamp and Childress 'principlism' framework; Beauchamp and Childress, 2001). This means that patients in their care should be treated neither as 'favourites' nor as 'outcasts'. This is also reflected in the Code of Professional Conduct (NMC, 2004).

Disability discrimination

A disabled person is defined in Section 1(2) – 'a person who has a disability':

> *If he or she has a physical or mental impairment which has a substantial and long term adverse effect on his or her ability to carry out normal day to day activities.*
> ### Section 1 (1) The Disability Discrimination Act (DDA) 1995

Owing to their physical and possible mental incapacity, a large number of patients may fall into this category, often being impaired (from a physical or mental incapacity) or having limited ability to function. This is an important area of law which the nurse needs to understand as they provide care for this group of (disabled) patients. It is the impairment of any part or parts of the body on which disability focuses (WHO, 2002). It is this impairment and the absence of or limitation of 'bodily mechanism' (Oliver, in Helman, 2001, p.23) that is seen by some as the basis for determining the presence of disability. For the purposes of government agencies, such as social services and the department of employment, any persons who are disabled were covered by the Disabled Persons Act 1944 Section 1 classification of those with the following:

> *(1) These include injury, disease or congenital deformity, is substantially handicapped in obtaining or keeping employment, or in undertaking work on his own account, of a kind which would be suited to his age, experience and qualifications.*

The DDA 1995, Section 20(1), suggests that discrimination exists when there is 'less favourable treatment' of a person with disability. The Disability Discrimination Act 2005 is a consolidation of the DDA 1995, and focuses on areas such as public transport and housing provision by regulating public authorities to ensure they treat all users fairly. Disability also includes mental illness under the Mental Health Act 1983, Section 1, which includes the following four categories:

1. mental illness;

2. mental impairment;

3. severe mental impairment;

4. psychopathic disorder.

Age discrimination

The National Service Framework (NSF) for Older People recognizes that elderly people may be discriminated against and sets a benchmark for healthcare professionals to aspire towards when delivering care for elderly people. This is a requirement for Standard 1 (Rooting out age discrimination) of the NSF for the Elderly (Department of Health, 2001).

> *NHS services will be provided, regardless of age, on the basis of clinical needs alone. Social care services will not use age in their eligibility criteria or policies, to restrict access to available services.*

The aim of NSFs such as the above is to improve national standards and hence the quality of care for patients. Breach of such standards does not mean an automatic breach of statutory provisions. However, where a trust fails to meet these standards, this may be evidence of liability in law, as when they fail in their duty of care to the patient in areas such as tort law. An example of an important aspect of discrimination which may affect the elderly in the provision of care is the provision of care packages. It is possible that this may be seen as a soft target in the need to save money, and effectively discriminates against the elderly. Discrimination takes place as a result of providers having stigma and prejudice. Prejudice has been defined above, on p. 113.

The nurse responsible for the care of an older person should never make assumptions, based on physical appearance and impairments alone, that the patient lacks mental capacity and will therefore be unaware of discrimination.

Racial discrimination

In most instances the concept of 'discrimination' takes many forms, with a range of definitions. The difficulty of racial discrimination is that it depends on a subjective element concerning the victim of the alleged racist act.

> *A person discriminates against another in any circumstances relevant for the purposes of any provision of this Act if*
>
> - *on racial grounds he treats that other less favourably than he treats or would treat other persons; or*
> - *he applies to that other a requirement or condition which he applies or would apply equally to persons not of the same racial group as that other.*
>
> ### Race Relations Acts 1976, Section 1

The onus or burden of proof is on the defendant to show that there was no unfair treatment on grounds of racism. When patients lack either mental or physical capacity, it may be very difficult to establish discrimination on the grounds of race. Discrimination on the grounds of race may also result from indirect discrimination by way of victimization.

A study by Shah and Priestley (2001) showed that subjects who came from black and ethnic minority backgrounds had experienced discriminatory practices while receiving care. They perceived this to be based on their race when they compared their treatment with that of others.

OTHER LESS COMMON TYPES OF DISCRIMINATION

It is difficult to establish how widespread other types of discrimination are in healthcare. This is because vulnerable people may be unwilling or unable to make a complaint under legislation such as the articles in Schedule 1 of the HRA Act 1998. This includes discrimination on grounds such as gender, sexual orientation and religious beliefs. Discrimination on grounds of gender is forbidden in the Equality Act 2006, while discrimination on the grounds of sexual orientation is also an issue following the passing of the Civil Partnership Act 2004, which now allows same sex partnerships to be recognized by law, affording individuals the same rights as a married couple. Discrimination on religion or on religious belief is now also outlawed under the Employment Equality (Religion or Belief) Regulations 2003.

The law (under the Equality Act 2006) now recognizes all the above aspects and contexts of discrimination. It is hoped that nurses can now turn to their own ethics, their professional code of conduct, national benchmarks such as the NSF for Older People and their local policies and guidelines which should all enshrine equal rights to fair treatment and care for all patients.

THINKING POINT

Jane is a young staff nurse who has worked on an acute care of the elderly ward for one year, post-qualifying. Two patients, Mrs Sand and Mrs Thomas, who both happen to be members of her place of worship, also speak the same language as Jane. She considers them both good friends. She decides not to tell other staff members. However, it has soon becomes clear that there is some 'friendship' between Jane and these two patients. Other patients have noticed and made comments to the effect that Jane spends more time talking to Mrs Sand and Mrs Thomas. She had been bringing in feature magazines for the two patients but not for the other patients. Sara, who is one of her colleagues working on the ward, has also noticed this.

1. Find out about your organization's anti-discrimination policies.
2. Based on this information, what advice would you give to Sara and Jane?

GROUNDS FOR DISCRIMINATION AND THE LAW TODAY

Owing to the difficulty in amassing such evidence it is only possible for the purposes of this chapter to have focused on three areas, which are those likely to have been experienced by patients within a caring environment. However reprehensible the concept of discrimination per se may sound, there is in fact no automatic recognition of it by the law; the law recognizes discrimination only within certain defined parameters. It could be argued that ethical or moral principles would dictate otherwise. Through legislation, parliament has defined and reinforced grounds for discrimination (EA 2006). This is an attempt to consider all forms of discrimination under the same umbrella. In reality, it is more probably based on anecdotal evidence only that some types of discrimination will be more common than others. Section 9 of the EA states that the Equality Commission will be mainly one of promoting and 'encouraging', without powers of enforcement, and is perhaps one of the weaknesses of the law in the area of discrimination.

THINKING POINT

A, aged 60, is a former GP, having retired 10 years ago due to ill health. He emigrated to the UK 10 years ago from another European country, soon after suffering a nervous breakdown following the ending of his previous relationship. He is admitted to a busy surgical ward for a routine total knee replacement operation. His operation went well though his rehabilitation is being hampered by the following problems:

- He is partially sighted and hard of hearing, which makes him highly dependent on nursing staff for carrying out everyday activities. As he is in a side room, he is always left until last for washing and dressing. He recently overhead the physiotherapist telling the occupational therapist that 'these foreigners are not very good at rehabilitation'.
- Dr A has been depressed since his lover of 10 years (a younger man, who was 20 years his junior) had recently left him for another man. This morning, a male staff nurse refused, for unspecified reasons, to give personal care without saying why.

How would you advise ward staff?
Consider the issues which you think may amount to discrimination.

CONCLUSION

Unfair or unequal treatment of patients could be perceived as discrimination. The Equalities Commission has as its objective the promotion of equality and diversity in all aspects of life (EA 2006, Section 8). The problem with discrimination is that under present UK law, the alleged victim has to make a claim about what they may perceive as discrimination. This may not pose any difficulty for patients who have the mental capacity. For those who lack capacity, however, they may be unaware of any discriminatory acts affecting their care, hence the importance of the Mental Capacity Act 2005 to safeguard their interests.

On the issue of diversity and equality, nurses as professionals should recognize that there are differences among the people who are their patients. Their patients are entitled to non-discriminatory treatment under human rights legislation and in ethics. While some differences may be visible, others may not be, which means that making assumptions about a patient's capacity or their needs can never be justified as these may result in discrimination. The standard of care nurses deliver should be influenced not purely by the law and by their own ethical beliefs but also by a professional culture, which recognizes and values patients as individuals. They should always respect the patient's human rights. Together, the EA (2006), the Race Relations (Amendment) Act 2000, the DDA 2005 and related statutes should make it easier for healthcare providers and others such as social services to have an integrated approach to the fair treatment of users in the elimination of discrimination.

REFERENCES

Beauchamp T, Childress J. *Bioethics*, 5th edn. Oxford: Oxford University Press, 2001.

Department of Health. *National Service Framework for Older People*, 2001, www.dh.gov.uk/en/Policyandguidance, accessed 18/07/07.

Jefferson T. Rough Draft of the American Declaration of Independence. In: Boyd J (ed.) *Papers of Thomas Jefferson*. Princeton, NJ: Princeton University Press, 1950: p.423.

Joint Committee on Human Rights Sixth Report, Session 2002–03, *The Case for a Human Rights Commission*, HL Paper 67-I and II, HC 489-I.

Nursing and Midwifery Council. *Code of professional conduct and ethics*. London, NMC, 2004.

Oliver M. In: Helman C (ed.) *Culture, health and illness*, 4th edition. London: Hodder Arnold, 2001: p.23.

Shah S, Priestley M. *Better services, better health: the healthcare experiences of black and minority ethnic disabled people*, 2001. www.leeds.ac.uk/disability-studies, accessed 20/02/07.

Twitchin J, Demuth C. *Multi-cultural education: Views from the classroom*, 2nd edn. London: BBC, 1985.

United Nations. UN General Assembly resolution 217 A (III), 10 December 1948, www.un.org, accessed 20/02/07.

United Nations. *The Universal Declaration of Human Rights*, 1948, www.un.org/Overview/rights.html, accessed 20/07/07.

World Health Organization. *Towards a Common Language for Functioning, Disability and Health International Classification of Functioning (ICF)*, 2002, www.who.int/medicines_technologies/human_rights/en/, accessed 16/11/07.

8 THEFT, FRAUD AND DECEPTION: PATIENTS' PROPERTY

INTRODUCTION

The topic under discussion is sometimes included under the general heading of 'abuse' when considering vulnerable individuals. It is important for the nurse to recognize and understand the nature of theft. The principle of theft in criminal law is the same, whether the theft is from the employer or from vulnerable patients. At times, this may pose some difficulty in cases of abuse when breach of the patient's human rights may include property rights. As the effect is not always obvious until discovery, this offence may go undetected for some time, especially in the case of vulnerable patients. This chapter also considers the grey areas where gifts may be inappropriate. Theft and fraud are both criminal law offences and are best addressed as separate entities from the general 'abuse' heading.

The standard definition of theft is

> *A person is guilty of theft if he dishonestly appropriates property belonging to another with the intention of permanently depriving the other of it and 'thief' and 'steal' shall be construed accordingly.*
> ### Section 1, Theft Act 1968

Property is defined as

> *(1) 'Property' includes money and all other property, real or personal, including things in action and other intangible property.*
> ### Section 4(1), Theft Act 1968

In law, the term property should be taken in the broadest sense (Dennis, 2003). This will also include a person's financial affairs such as money and shares. As a professional, the NMC code of professional conduct expects that the nurse be trustworthy as part of their duty of care (NMC, 2004). Most trusts have a clear policy of safeguarding patients' property. As their capacity may be impaired through illness, a patient may easily lose their valuable property without being aware.

In most people's minds, there exists a very clear concept of the moral obligations and implications of an owner's rights, and of 'theft' and its impact on society at large. Beyond the ordinary meaning of ethics or a consensus of moral connotations of 'theft' in most societies, this word is also associated with fraudulent behaviour, deliberate deception or a lack of probity, dishonesty, cheating and lying. Also, the use of some undue influence in order to gain advantage of another person, especially where there is a breach of trust as in a caring relationship, may amount to the generic term of 'theft'.

The letter of the law may be followed in the court's ability to redress the imbalance by punishing the offender and/or compensating the victim. Punishment of the perpetrator is achieved indirectly in criminal law by paying their (the offender's) debt to society although not automatically providing the victim of crime with direct redress. The victim may be awarded compensation through the Criminal Injuries Compensation Authority if there is any injury associated with the crime. In addition, they may also seek damages for personal injuries through the civil courts themselves. A victim who feels that justice has not been done may pursue a private criminal prosecution. Unfortunately this may prove difficult and costly for most people.

A nurse or other carer may resort to theft or fraudulent behaviour, if motivated by corruption, greed or simply a lack of moral consideration, principles or integrity. The use of different terminology, i.e. 'theft' or 'fraud' to describe what could be the same crime, may lead to confusion, even for the courts, as is demonstrated by the case of *Ghosh* below.

THEFT OR FRAUD

In criminal law, a crime consists of two elements, namely the *mens rea*, 'a guilty mind', and the *actus reus*, 'a guilty act'. It is a prerequisite for both elements to be present for any crime to be established (Jefferson, 2001). The main elements of the above offences are similar but not identical. The elements of theft will be discussed more specifically.

The act of theft involves coming into possession of goods belonging to another without the knowledge or permission of the owner. This paints a picture of goods being obtained by stealth or secretively, that is without the overt knowledge of the owner. The *mens rea* or guilty intention is 'dishonesty' and 'the intention to permanently deprive' the other. The *actus reus* or guilty act of theft is 'the appropriation of property belonging to another'.

Fraud, on the other hand, is usually more discrete, but achieved through deception, trickery or under 'false pretences'. Goods are handed over to the perpetrator, usually with the knowledge and apparent 'consent' of the victim. The problem is that if the respondent can prove that this consent was given by a person who is deemed by the court to be 'of sound mind' then there is no guilty mind and therefore no crime of fraud or theft. On the other hand, if a nurse has acquired an 'inappropriate gift' or 'loan' from a patient or their representatives, even if this was with the owner's permission, they may be in breach of paragraphs 7.4 and 7.5 of the professional code of conduct (NMC, 2004).

The guilty intention and the guilty act for the fraud offence are very similar to the ones for theft, apart from the way this is achieved. The result is the same. These offences fall under the provisions in Sections 1 and 15 of the Theft Act 1968, respectively. Where a defendant to a charge of theft alleges that in assuming the right to the property, they believed that the owner did consent to the 'appropriation' of goods, they may find themselves facing a charge not of 'theft' but of 'fraud' under Section 3 of the 1968 act. The principle is illustrated in the following case in Fionda and Bryant (2000, p.59–60).

R v Ghosh (1982) 75 CR App. R. 154

A surgeon who was acting as a locum consultant at a hospital falsely represented that he had carried out surgical operations and claimed payment. Someone else under the NHS had in fact carried out the operations. The defendant was convicted of obtaining property by deception.

The Court of Appeal held that 'In determining whether the defendant was acting dishonestly, the jury had first to consider whether, according to the standards of the ordinary reasonable person, what was done was dishonest. If it was, the jury must then consider whether D himself must have realised that what he was doing was dishonest by the standards of the ordinary reasonable person'.

Within a caring environment, it is possible for a vulnerable patient to be subjected to fraud rather than theft, although theft is also possible. The effect nevertheless is the same – a breach of patients' rights to their property.

Fraud is usually carried out through deception or dishonesty, which means that it is possible to establish the owner's consent. The owner is somehow tricked or misled by some action into giving up their property for the benefit of the thief. This aspect of the theft offence is now covered by Section 15A of the Theft Act. This section was inserted by the Theft (Amendment) Act 1996. It provides for a person to be guilty of an offence if, 'by deception they dishonestly obtain a money transfer for himself or another and included false accounting'. Additionally obtaining a pecuniary advantage by deception falls under s16 Theft Act 1968. The obtaining of services by deception and evasion of liability by deception fall under s1 Theft Act 1978 and s2 Theft Act 1978, respectively. The principle of law that has come to be known as the 'Ghosh test' was first applied in *R* v *Ghosh* (1982).

While theft, on conviction, carries a maximum prison sentence of seven years, fraud can invoke a longer term of ten years. The heavier sentence is reflected by the fact that fraud often involves higher and substantial sums of money or property and it may be difficult to detect the crime especially if the money or assets have been spent by the time the fraud is discovered. The effect on the victim, nevertheless, is likely to be the same.

A British crime survey (2005–6) showed that 29 per cent of crime was 'other theft'. When broken down as recorded by the police, it was shown that while 'other crime' accounted for 23 per cent of the crime, fraud and forgery amounted to 4 per cent. The Law Revision Committee (1968) acknowledged the difficulty of recognizing theft (Jefferson, 2001).

THE NURSE, MORALITY AND PATIENTS' PROPERTY RIGHTS

Moral philosophy tries to set the boundaries for merits or demerits of certain human actions such as theft or fraud. Professional ethics follow these and would view any justification of theft or fraud involving disadvantaged patients not only as unacceptable but as 'unprofessional', in no uncertain terms. Consensus in most societies would agree that theft should never be condoned and there is no doubt that this is a violation of individual rights. When patients are ill, they may lack the capacity for decision-making or simply lack any will to safeguard their own rights. Incapacity may be temporary, for example due to the environment or the medication, or permanent which may be due to ageing or to disease processes. They should therefore expect nurses to whose care they are entrusted to 'be trustworthy' and 'act to identify and minimise risk to patients and clients' (NMC, 2004, paragraph 7).

Nurses and other healthcare professionals are obliged to consult their professional codes of conduct for direction as well as relevant local policies and guidelines in order to ensure that a patient's property rights are not eroded. In a criminal court, the evidence in the areas of the theft and fraud offences can prove to be difficult to establish as this may take part in secret. In response, a defendant may allege that they honestly,

> (a) *believed that they had a legal right to deprive the victim of the property.*
> (b) *believes the victim would have consented to the appropriation of the property if he had known of the circumstances.*
> (c) *finds or otherwise appropriates property when he believes that the owner, possessor or controller cannot be reasonably be found.*
> ### Section 2(1), Theft Act 1968

It may be difficult to establish theft due to the relationship of trust. This trust, however, is open to abuse as the following case illustrates, where a nursing home matron swindled sick and dying patients out of more than £100 000 to fund her extravagant luxury lifestyle. 'X' treated herself to exotic holidays, designer clothes and hundreds of pounds of jewellery as she bled dry the bank accounts of her terminally ill and mentally handicapped patients (*Daily Mail*, 2006).

While the nurse is expected to maintain professional boundaries within a therapeutic relationship, the fact of the matter is that this may sometimes be compromised by a close relationship with a patient or their next of kin. It is important therefore that while advocating for the patient, nurses maintain a neutral position and maintain professional boundaries. Should they suspect a colleague of deception, through fraudulently obtaining property from a patient, or by accepting inappropriate gifts from patients, they have a duty to report it.

THINKING POINT

Mrs X, aged 78, was admitted from home following a collapse, to the same medical ward where her husband had been a patient for many months previously. The couple are childless and have been married for 54 years. The ambulance paramedics handed in three deposit account bankbooks containing substantial sums and a holdall with £18 655 in cash – they asked the police to check the total of their 'discovery'. Mrs X, who is not normally
(Continued)

confused, now says that £3000 of her money is missing. The only people with access to her property are a distant but seemingly caring niece and 'friendly and very helpful' neighbours, a young couple in their thirties. They are both unemployed, and Mrs X's niece who is the next-of-kin (and who lives abroad) is worried that the neighbours have been spending a lot of time at her auntie's house doing domestic chores. Mrs X also said that over time valuable ornaments had gone missing but because her neighbours had been so good to her she did not want to cause any trouble.

1. Examine your Trust's policy on patients' property.
2. In the above case, consider what action you would take.

GIFTS, STRINGS ATTACHED AND PROFESSIONAL ETHICS

The issue of accepting gifts is not always clear-cut for some healthcare professionals, for example research by Levene and Stirling (1980, cited in Lyckholm, 1998) found that 20 per cent of doctors from different specialties admitted receiving gifts from patients. Nurses, however, as healthcare professionals are expected to respect the patient's property and not take any personal rewards.

> *7.4 You must refuse any gift, favour, or hospitality that might be interpreted, now or in the future, as an attempt to obtain preferential consideration.*
>
> *7.5 You must neither ask for nor accept loans from patients, clients or their relatives and friends.*
>
> **NMC (2004)**

The danger in accepting gifts, often given as a sign of appreciation of the care that has been given, is that even if the patient's intention is genuine, it is possible that a healthcare professional who accepts 'gifts' from a patient they have been looking after, may subsequently find their position compromised. A conflict of interests may arise and when clinical judgements are required to be made, they may be expected to return 'favours' or to give the patient preferential treatment. A difficult situation is created when such gifts are given in advance of treatment. It is often difficult to draw the line between the usual festive 'box of chocolates for the nurses' as a blanket donation to all staff and specific gifts aimed at individual nurses (Griffith, 2003). On the other hand, gifts which are given for the benefit of a group of staff are probably easier to reconcile with the standards expected of a registered nurse in this area (NMC, 2004). In addition, there will be Trust policies in place, breach of which may result in disciplinary action for the nurse who accepts individual gifts from patients.

The therapeutic relationship between a nurse and a patient is based on trust and this may put patients in a position that is open to exploitation. It is important therefore that the nurse's relationship with patients should be seen to have transparency at all times (Dudley, 2002).

CAPACITY AND PROTECTING THE PATIENT'S PROPERTY RIGHTS

Some patients may be physically or psychologically dependent, and may therefore become a potential victim of theft or fraud from carers. A lack of capacity to consent may also impact on capacity to manage their property. A confused patient is more vulnerable when it comes to safe storage and custody of their property. Hence, the nurse should follow their local policy to ensure that when their (patients') property rights are threatened, they should be prepared to act, insofar as is reasonably practicable and to the best of their knowledge. This threat may come from a patient's family, friends or colleagues. It is the financial aspect where patients are most vulnerable. While there is generally a presumption in law that every individual adult and child should be allowed to make decisions involving their financial assets, it has often been the case that some patients may not be in a position to do so due to their physical or mental incapacity. Such a vulnerable person may therefore be at risk of theft or fraud involving money or other property (Langan, cited in Brayne and Carr, 2003).

As a key healthcare professional, the nurse should be able to identify any signs of financial or property abuse. The patient may choose to confide in them or they may witness in conversation with people close to the patient that something unusual has taken place. The difficulty a nurse has in reporting fraud may be the lack of evidence. Nevertheless, when they have reasonable suspicion of theft or fraud it is best to voice their concerns to senior colleagues or their line manager and document this fact, in case it is required as evidence in future. Other members of the multidisciplinary team should also be involved in any ensuing investigation. Owing to their statutory powers and function, a social worker is usually the key person to lead the process of investigation and reporting. They may resort to informal or formal methods for protection of victims of theft or fraud (Brayne and Carr, 2003). Their main objective may be described as 'seeking to safeguard and promote the rights and interest of service users whenever possible' (British Association of Social Workers, paragraph 4.1.1(c)).

Several remedies are open to the social worker and these may be formal or informal. Informal protection measures can be implemented with the agreement of the patient, family members and multidisciplinary team members where theft or fraud is suspected. Often this saves time and 'red tape' before going down the formal route; it is best to follow local policies or guidelines (which must take cognizance of the law), in ensuring that the patient's best interests are served. The government introduced the Protection of Vulnerable Adults (POVA) Guidance in July 2004 and the Protection of Vulnerable Groups (Scotland) Bill (2006), with the aim of protecting vulnerable adults (aged 18 years and above) in care settings in both England and Wales. This requires social services departments up and down the country to hold an offenders' register, which can disclose any individual's history of abuse to employers. This is in addition to the Criminal Records Bureau, which is run by the Home Office. In practice, it may be quite difficult to gather evidence if the victim is unwilling to make a complaint (due to fear of victimization or if they lack the capacity to do so). The protection of children comes under separate legislation and this is dealt with in Chapter 4, Children's rights – the beginning of life to the age of majority. The priority should be to support the victims before and during the prosecution of the perpetrator.

One appropriate response to suspected financial/property abuse is by the compulsory removal of an incapacitated victim to a place of safety if:

> (a) *they are suffering from grave chronic disease or being aged, infirm or physically incapacitated, are living in unsanitary conditions and*
> (b) *are unable to devote to themselves ... are not receiving from other persons, proper care and attention.*
> ### Section 47, National Assistance Act 1948

This could then make it more difficult for any fraud to continue. For individuals with mental incapacity, Section 94(2) of the Mental Health Act 1983 defines a 'patient' as 'a person who on medical evidence is incapable, by reason of mental disorder, of managing and administering his property and affairs'. Over a period of time, the courts have seen as one of their roles, the protection of rights of those who lack mental capacity. As a result the system of receivership has been developed, which allows the court to appoint an appropriate person who may be a solicitor, spouse or family member who has cared for a patient, a local authority employee or a friend, to manage their affairs (Rule 7(1) of the Court of Protection Rules 2001). This person is accountable to the courts and is required to submit financial reports periodically.

The Mental Capacity Act 2005 (MCA 2005) came into force from April 2007 thus empowering patients and strengthening current rules. The equivalent Scottish statute is the Adults with Incapacity (Scotland) Act 2000. Under the MCA 2005 the guiding principles for determining capacity are:

(1) The following principles apply for the purposes of this Act.

(2) A person must be assumed to have capacity unless it is established that he lacks capacity.

(3) A person is not to be treated as unable to make a decision unless all practicable steps to help him to do so have been taken without success.

(4) A person is not to be treated as unable to make a decision merely because he makes an unwise decision.

(5) An act done or decision made, under this Act for or on behalf of a person who lacks capacity must be done, or made, in his best interests.

(6) Before the act is done, or the decision is made, regard must be had to whether the purpose for which it is needed can be as effectively achieved in a way that is less restrictive of the person's rights and freedom of action.

Section 1, MCA 2005

THINKING POINT

Mrs X is a 50-year-old widow who has suffered from multiple sclerosis for the last six years and is increasingly become dependent on four carers for personal hygiene. She is sometimes incontinent and needs helps with washing and dressing, requiring care twice a day. Her son, who lives abroad, recently suspects that Angela, who is one of her trusted regular carers, has been regularly withdrawing large sums of money without his mother's consent and she does not always provide receipts for shopping. Unbeknown to the son, Angela has a criminal record but has managed to get this job through an agency, which failed to check her credentials on engaging her.

What advice would you give to Mrs X's son?

The MCA 2005 is applicable on assessment of a person's capacity, which should be based on a 'decision-specific' test.

- *A presumption of capacity – every adult has the right to make his or her own decisions and must be assumed to have capacity to do so unless it is proved otherwise.*

- *The right for individuals to be supported to make their own decisions – people must be given all appropriate help before anyone concludes that they cannot make their own decisions.*
- *That individuals must retain the right to make what might be seen as eccentric or unwise decisions.*
- *Best interests – anything done for or on behalf of people without capacity must be in their best interests.*
- *Least restrictive intervention – anything done for or on behalf of people without capacity should be the least restrictive of their basic rights and freedoms.*

Section 1 Mental Capacity Act 2005

There is now no presumption of incapacity based on a patient's medical condition or state of mind (Section 2, MCA 2005). In any decision-making where the patient lacks capacity their 'best interests' must be considered. The above principles are seen as key to providing new safeguards for people lacking in capacity.

One example of protection of the vulnerable patient (who lacks capacity) based on Scots Law is the Mental Health (Care and Treatment) (Scotland) Act 2003. Guardianship is addressed in Chapter 5, Section 7, which states that the Guardian, and only the Guardian her/himself, has the power to:

- require the person to live at a particular place;
- require the person to go to specific places at specific times for the purpose of medical treatment.

Nevertheless, subject to Section 94(2) of the Mental Health Act 1983,

2) The functions of the judge under this Part of this Act shall be exercisable where, after considering medical evidence. he is satisfied that a person is incapable, by reason of mental disorder, of managing and administering his property and affairs; and a person as to whom the judge is so satisfied is referred to in this Part of this Act as a patient.

This section would also allow a judge to administer a decision regarding administering such a patient's property under Section 95 of that act.

Section 46 of the MCA (2005) brings new provisions for the Court of Protection, giving special wider powers to the Court of Protection for deciding on matters related to a patient's incapacity. In the same vein, the Mental Health Bill 2007 aims to ensure treatment of those who need treatment while improving the protection of individuals who lack capacity.

For those with mental capacity, they may choose to appoint a financial 'advocate' to manage their affairs when they lack the capacity to choose. There are two main categories: ordinary power of attorney and lasting power of attorney.

Ordinary power of attorney

In this category, a person may choose any person whom they so wish to represent them. When the patient loses their capacity for decision-making, a representative to whom such power is delegated subsequently has the power to make decisions on their behalf. In law, there is a presumption that any decisions they make will be in the best interests of the person they represent. In addition, the person who delegates this power may revoke this power at any time.

Lasting power of attorney

A solicitor is normally required for verifying the wishes of the person drawing up a legal deed and their capacity to do so. A person chosen to manage their financial affairs will have the right to carry out any necessary transactions should the person drawing up the deed lose their mental capacity. The physical or mental incapacity may be due to illness.

Court of Protection (Sections 93–98 Mental Health Act 1983)

This is required for individuals who lack mental capacity and is the most appropriate route for safeguarding their interests. An application to the court must be supported by consultant medical opinion in the relevant documents of the patient's state of mind. If the court accepts this, it appoints a 'receiver' who is answerable to the court. One way of safeguarding the interests of a vulnerable person is the requirement for accounts to be submitted to the court periodically. The Court of Protection has, nevertheless, not without criticism, been seen as 'archaic, bureaucratic, and disempowering' (Lush, 2001, p.239).

Department of Work and Pensions, welfare benefits representative

For a person who is on welfare benefits, it is possible for the Department of Work and Pensions to appoint a representative, who may be any person, for example a social worker or one of their employees, to be representative in respect of a client's payments. This is a quick and relatively easy way to protect the patient, although there is the risk of fraud since no medical opinion is required as evidence for representation of a client who may be vulnerable.

CONCLUSION

Theft brings to mind the concept of being perpetrated by strangers, through 'stealth'; while fraud should more easily be noticed or suspected by clinicians due to 'unusual arrangements'. It is a fact of life nevertheless that fraudulent or dishonest acts of appropriation take place because of the imbalance of power in relation to vulnerable patients. The effect is a breach of the patient's rights. Worse still for the patient may be the long-term effects of the trauma if this breach is in a therapeutic relationship and by someone they trusted. The likelihood of the crime of theft or fraud within a caring relationship is real; the temptation to accept inappropriate gifts is also real. Property-related offences comprise a substantial proportion of crime, hence the need to intervene on behalf of the patient, especially where they are vulnerable. The challenge for the nurse, therefore, is that 'it is the respectable offender who provides the most interesting illustration of why and how fraudsters frequently care not to be perceived as real criminals' (Ashe and Counsel 1993, p.178, cited in Wilson, 2006). The worrying thing is that the real extent of these problems may never be known due to victims' reluctance or inability to report the matter. It is therefore important for health authorities to ensure that robust policies are in place to safeguard the property rights of patients, especially those who are vulnerable.

REFERENCES

Brayne H, Carr H. *Law for social workers*, 8th edn. Oxford: Oxford University Press, 2003.

British Association of Social Workers Code of Ethics, 2003, paragraph 4.1.1(c) www.basw.co.uk.

Daily Mail. 2006. www.dailymail.co.uk/pages/live/articles/news/ news.html? in_article_id = 401506&in_page_id = 1770.

Department of Constitutional Affairs. 2007. www.dca.gov.uk/search.htm.

Department of Health. www.dh.gov.uk, accessed 20/07/07.

Dennis I. *Criminal law statutes 2003/04*, 6th edn. London: Thompson Sweet & Maxwell, 2003.

Dudley N. Dishonest doctors should not continue to practise. *BMJ* 2002; **324**: 547.

Fionda J, Bryant M. *Brief case criminal law*, 2nd edn. London: Cavendish Publishing, 2000.

Griffith R. Generosity or stealing? When accepting a gift can be theft. *British Journal of Community Nursing* 2003; **8**: 512–14.

Jefferson M. *Criminal law*, 5th edn. London: Longman, 2001.

Home Office. *Crime in England and Wales 2005–6: A summary of the main statistics*, HOSB 12/06 Home Office, 2006, www.homeoffice.gov.uk/rds/crimeew0506.html.

Lyckholm L. Should physicians accept gifts from patients? *Journal of American Medical Association* 1998; **280**: 1994–6.

Lush D. Partnership in action. In: Roche J, Cull L-A (eds). *The law, social work practice and elder abuse*. Basingstoke: Palgrave, 2001.

Nursing and Midwifery Council. *Professional code of conduct and ethics*. London: NMC, 2004.

Wilson S. Law, morality and regulations: victimization experiences of financial crime. *British Journal of Criminology* 2006; **46**: 1073–90.

INTRODUCTION – LIFE AT THE END DECISIONS

Human mortality is an indisputable fact, and this is based on everyday experience. To most people, 'Dying is a human process in the same way that being born is a normal and all-human process' (Kubler-Ross, 1991, p.10). Nowadays, it is much more difficult to determine when death occurs due to advanced medical science interventions (Campbell *et al.*, 2001). The core ethical question on the end of life issue is how and when the end of life may be allowed. Death is difficult to determine, 'as a result of developments in modern medical technology, doctors no longer associate death exclusively with breathing and heart beat, and it has come to be accepted that death occurs when the brain, and in particular the brain stem, has been destroyed' (Lord Goff in the following case).

Airedale NHS Trust v Bland [1993] 1 All ER 821

Anthony David Bland, a Liverpool Football Club fan, then aged 17, attended the Hillsborough ground for a match. During the disastrous course of events of that day, he was crushed and subsequently suffered brain damage from a lack of oxygen supply to his brain, with resulting irreversible brain

---

damage. By the time the case went to court, he had been in a persistent vegetative state (PVS) for some time. The question for the court was whether his artificial feeding should be discontinued, and with the agreement of the consultant and the family, this was allowed.

The definitions of 'life' and 'death' are the subject of debate throughout healthcare professional frameworks. There are both ends of the spectrum – on the one hand, absolute preservation of life (and delaying the inevitable) and on the other hand, allowing death or 'letting go', if not assisting or hastening the end. In either case, there is a potential conflict of interests, between the patient's best interests versus those of society as a whole. Society's motives may be driven either by caring and altruistic concerns to prolong life, or (cynically) economic reasons may play a part, by considering the costs of maintaining what seems to be a futile life. What is also important in the above case is the court's finding that there is no absolute obligation on doctors to prolong life regardless of the outcome.

Under certain provisions, states assume their right through legislation to determine when a life can be ended, actively or passively. This may be in the case of retributive justice, when a capital sentence is allowed for murder, on the basis of the 'life for life' principle. Sometimes in law justifiable homicide (one person killing another) will be accepted, but this is only in clearly defined circumstances.

When applied to the clinical setting, it is a reasonable expectation in civil law and in ethics that healthcare professionals owe a duty of care to provide a reasonable standard of care to maintain the welfare of patients under their care (*Donaghue* v *Stevenson* [1932], AC 532; discussed below). Their primary goal should be to promote health as well as to save lives. A dilemma may arise when healthcare professionals must engage in end of life decisions. Healthcare professionals may experience contrasting roles, from fighting to save a life to accepting the fact that treatment may be futile with death being inevitable. It has been suggested that 'nurses have to implement ethical decisions to withdraw treatment when they have not been party to the decision making process' (Viney, 1996, p.182) in the first place. The most important ethical question is to determine whether in their role they can foresee circumstances in which it is justifiable to either actively or passively terminate that life by withdrawing treatment.

The Ancient Greeks believed that there might be situations in which euthanasia would be acceptable provided that it was 'easy and gentle'. The word 'euthanasia' had a somewhat wider connotation then, having no specific reference to so-called 'mercy killing' (Teichman, 1996, p.65). In consideration of patient care by physicians, the Hippocratic oath (500BC) required physicians to sustain and enhance the quality of life of their patients. These are related to a general consensus evident in professional codes of conduct across disciplines of healthcare professionals. This means that most ethical philosophies and religions view life as a gift from a supernatural 'being', some form of deity or from 'Mother Nature'. This entity is seen as having the ultimate right to give or to take life. There is, however, no consensus at what stage life begins and equally no agreement as to when life should end. Medical science can now sustain life at a basic level to a greater extent than in the time of the Ancient Greeks. Incidentally, the legal definition of death is much broader, to include biological life, while the clinical-medical one is limited to brain stem dysfunction as the basis for determining death, a persistent vegetative state (PVS). The law on human rights takes into account the fact that every patient is entitled to a right to life (Article 2, Human Rights Act 1998), hence this has been used as a basis for litigation to assert that right.

> *Everyone's right to life shall be protected by the law. No one shall be deprived of his life intentionally save in the execution of a sentence of a court following his conviction of a crime for which this penalty is provided by the law.*
>
> **Article 2, Human Rights Act 1998**

This nevertheless should be qualified. There are many definitions of euthanasia and the preferred one serves as a starting point for defining euthanasia as

> *An easy and painless death, mercy killing*
>
> **Dorland Medical Dictionary**

Another definition is:

> *The literary origin of the word 'Eu-thanasia' is the Greek translation for, a 'good- death'. It has been argued by some that the concept of euthanasia should include a positive 'enabling' aspect which includes the patient's autonomy and the right to choice.*
>
> **Davies (1998, p.344)**

Healthcare professionals, in general, and doctors, in particular, face a dilemma when trying to establish a patient's capacity to choose treatment which, in their professional judgement, they may consider to be futile. This task is difficult considering that a patient's judgement may be influenced by poor physical and/or psychological impairment resulting from disease. The ability to establish the patient's best interests is even more difficult when they (the patient) are totally mentally incapacitated or have intermittent spells of consciousness and rationality. The question posed here is whether there are any circumstances where substitution of that judgement by another person's judgement would be justifiable. There follows a definition of 'best interests' with an explanation for determining them.

> *(1) In determining for the purposes of this Act what is in a person's best interests, the person's best interests, the person making the determination must consider all the circumstances appearing to him to be relevant.*
> *(2) In particular, he must take the following steps.*
> *(3) He must consider (a) whether it is likely that the person will at some time have capacity in relation to the matter in question and, (b) if it appears likely that he will, when that is likely to be.*
> **Mental Capacity Bill 2004, paragraph 4**

CLASSIFICATION OF EUTHANASIA

Active euthanasia

An individual may legally take active measures to end their life by consuming a concoction of drugs or by any other means, knowing that that action will end their life, which is suicide. A similar effect may be achieved through the assistance of another person, in which case this becomes 'assisted suicide' as well as the crime of aiding and abetting (Section 2(1) Suicide Act 1961). These are offences subject to criminal law scrutiny and possible prosecution. Physician-assisted suicide is an alternative to withdrawal of treatment, when a patient requests a doctor to provide them with drugs that will shorten or end life. Euthanasia is murder in the UK. This is on the basis of the following case.

Regina v Cox (1992) 12 BMLR 38

A 70-year-old woman suffered from severe arthritis with severe pain. It could not be established how much longer she would have lived (but for the administration of a potent substance resulting in her death). She had suffered from severe arthritic pain for several years, which was not controlled by analgesia. She had requested her consultant, Cox to put her out of her misery. Dr Cox then knowingly injected her with a lethal dose of potassium chloride resulting in her death. He was initially charged with murder but subsequently found guilty of attempted murder. The judge directing the jury said that, 'if it is proved that Dr Cox injected Lillian Boyes with potassium chloride in circumstances which make sure that by that act he intended to kill her, then he is guilty of attempted murder'. The case resulted in a suspended sentence. As the body had been cremated before the case was brought to the attention of the police, it was not proven that the injected potassium was the cause of death.

Physician-assisted suicide may be either voluntary, in the case where a patient is mentally competent and gives permission, or it may be involuntary, where the patient lacks the capacity to make a choice, in the case of an unconscious patient. Incompetent patients have no legal rights to refuse consent to treatment. There are now new provisions under the Mental Capacity Act 2005, while the Mental Health Act 1983, is replaced by the Mental Health Act 2007, with Adults with Incapacity (Scotland) Act 2000, Mental Health (Care and Treatment) (Scotland) Act 2003 applicable, respectively. Unless it can be proven otherwise, there is now a presumption in law that every adult patient has the capacity to make an informed decision. The difference between 'suicide' and 'physician-assisted suicide' is that the latter is carried out within a clinical setting and protected by the law in only a handful of countries. Physician-assisted euthanasia is illegal under current UK legislation.

Passive euthanasia

This involves those situations in which a patient's treatment is either withdrawn by stopping current treatment or by making a decision that no new interventions will be instituted. One example is where antibiotics may be indicated for treatment of a chest infection and a conscious decision is made to not give antibiotics because any further treatment would not have any meaningful benefit to the patient. Since *Airedale* v *Bland* [1993], where there is a lack of clarity, the court's permission must be sought before making a decision to withdraw treatment.

Voluntary euthanasia

Voluntary euthanasia involves a patient who possesses the mental capacity to make an informed choice. Such a patient may choose to accept a form of treatment or to refuse it even with the awareness that the consequence will be detrimental to their health. A patient's right to exercise autonomy in accepting or refusing treatment should be respected in ethics. On this basis, in some countries, for example the Netherlands, voluntary physician-assisted suicide would be granted if the conditions for the relevant framework were satisfied. This is different in the UK, although the Mental Capacity Act 2005 England and Wales which implements the Convention on the International Protection of Adults (signed at The Hague on 13 January 2000 (Cm. 5881)) changes the balance in favour of the patient. On the other hand, doctors and nurses may not be forced to carry out any clinical actions they consider contrary to their professional judgement or which they find morally reprehensible unless this is within the confines of the law.

Involuntary euthanasia

Involuntary euthanasia applies to situations where a patient lacks the capacity to make a rational choice and this raises questions on the extent to which, in reality, a patient's autonomy can influence outcomes related to treatment. There has been long-standing provision for a formal proxy to make decisions on behalf of the patient in financial matters (the proxy having been granted a Power of Attorney), but not decisions on treatment. The power of the 'Healthcare Proxy' was different under Scottish law, where the former may, in certain circumstances, make a choice on behalf of the patient. Since the passing of the Mental Capacity Act 2005 however, a deputy in England and Wales and Northern Ireland now has similar powers. This introduces a new dimension and a presumption in law that every adult has the capacity to make an informed decision.

Adoption of an ethical framework for decision-making (which is considered as universal in its application) is necessary for healthcare professionals in order to reach the correct decisions related to the end of life. Principlism (or bioethical principles) aims to include autonomy, beneficence, non-maleficence, and fairness in the decision-making framework, making the four ethical principles an essential part of the medical/nursing ethical framework for decision-making. Beauchamp and Childress (1997) first termed them 'universal principles' or 'principlism' and added the first principle. Euthanasia from the above perspectives may be caused either by someone's own actions or the actions of others. An example of own actions is refusal of treatment, which may result in termination of life. The general principle of a patient's right to autonomy was, nevertheless, altered in the following case.

Re T (Adult: Refusal of Medical Treatment) [1992] 4 ALL ER 649, CA

A pregnant woman aged 20 had suffered serious injuries in a road traffic accident. The injuries included a haemorrhage, which resulted in the birth of a stillborn baby. She had been 34 weeks pregnant and, on admission, had consented to a Caesarean section. Her mother who was a strict Jehovah's Witness had then influenced her daughter who (Ms T) subsequently told doctors that she objected to a blood transfusion. Her boyfriend and his father on the other hand objected and sought a judicial review authorizing a blood transfusion as a life-saving measure. Held by the court of Appeal (Lord Donaldson's judgement) that:

1. Her mental capacity to choose whether to accept a blood transfusion or not had been impaired by her injuries.
2. She had lacked sufficient information to make an informed (rational) decision to accept or refuse treatment.
3. Undue pressure from her mother may have influenced her subsequent decision to appear to reject a blood transfusion.

The courts therefore could not apply the ethical principle of autonomy under these circumstances and ordered a transfusion to be given to Ms T without her consent.

SUICIDE – HUMAN RIGHT OR A CRIMINAL ACT?

The concept of 'human rights' presumes that every person may make a choice about how and where they lead their lives and therefore it follows that this right should include how and when to terminate their lives. Under Section 1, Suicide Act 1961 suicide is no longer a crime, meaning that prosecution will not follow but this provision does not mean that the UK sanctions the act of suicide. Other competing interests in society may limit individual rights and choices. A patient's expressed wish to commit suicide may be motivated by unbearable pain and/or depressive illness as well as by social pressures. Assisted suicide takes place when another person is involved, be it a doctor or a lay person.

> *A person who aids, abets, counsels or procures the suicide of another or an attempt by another to commit suicide shall be liable on conviction on indictment to imprisonment for a term not exceeding 14 years.*
> **Section 2(1), Suicide Act 1961**
> **(Butterworths, 2000)**

When a person assists another person to take their life, they may be charged with murder under Section 1 of the Homicide Act 1957. Under Section 4 of the same statute, however, where evidence of a suicide pact is present, the charge may be reduced from murder to manslaughter. Section 2(1) Suicide Act 1961 (above) sets a maximum sentence of 14 years' imprisonment. This section was unsuccessfully challenged in the case below.

***Pretty* v *The United Kingdom* [European Court of Human Rights], Application no. 2346/02, Strasbourg, April 29, [2002]**

In this case, a woman with motor neuron disease invoked her right to choose refusal of treatment, under Articles 3 and 8 of the European Convention on Human Rights 1950. She sought immunity from prosecution for her husband on assisting her to die with dignity. This was refused by the House of Lords and that decision was upheld by the European Court of Human Rights.

The mainstream religions such as Christianity, Islam and Judaism do not accept an individual's right to commit suicide on the basis of what is regarded as the 'sanctity of life'. Buddhism also rejects the notion of suicide or self-harm as morally reprehensible and wrong. Some Hindu writers would argue however that 'there is a right time (natural) "kala" for death' and also hold that there should be 'the acceptability of willed death, where a man may control his death by refusing to take food or drink' (Morgan and Lawton, 1996, p.3). They nevertheless believe that only the supernatural or 'Divine Being' has the right to give and take life. Some moral philosophers, for example Kant (1724–1804), propose that under no circumstance should suicide be justifiable. His 'categorical imperative' concept includes a moral duty to do what is right, and cannot include suicide, as this would be absurd. It is not a question of choice. On the other hand, utilitarianism would argue that whatever course of action produces the greatest benefit or happiness for the greatest number of people should be followed, and hence could justify suicide in some circumstances. From a pragmatic point of view, it could be argued that, at least for those with loved ones and dependants, suicide is an inconsiderate option. The views of other interested parties (for example loved ones) are often not considered. Attitudes towards life and death matters and how to deal with end of life decisions through euthanasia vary internationally and across Europe, as shown by one view on euthanasia.

Wherever a sick person in perfect clarity of mind demands strongly that an end be put to an existence which has lost all meaning for him and wherever a committee of doctors convoked for the purpose recognises the unavailability of any other treatment, euthanasia should be granted.

The EC Human Rights Commission (1991)

A recent ruling by the High Court redefined the meaning of withdrawal of treatment in the following case.

Burke v General Medical Council [2005] EWCA Civ 1003

A patient suffering from a degenerative brain disease effectively challenged the GMC Guidelines for deciding on withdrawal of treatment for a patient diagnosed as being in a persistent vegetative state. According to *The Times,* 'the ruling reflects a shift from the medical profession and into the hands of patients. It also however, forms part of a less welcome shift in power out of the hands of practitioners and into the hands of the courts' (*The Times*, 31 July 2004). The effect was to oblige the medical staff to continue with active (probably relatively expensive) treatment which some may see as futile, even though Mr Burke was considered to be in the terminal stages of life.

On appeal, the House of Lords and further the European Court of Human Rights held that doctors should not be expected to continue treatment of a patient (who suffered from muscle ataxia in this case) if in their judgement this was considered futile.

DO NOT ATTEMPT RESUSCITATION ORDERS

Here, examples of the terms commonly used are 'do not resuscitate', 'do not attempt resuscitation', 'not for resuscitation', 'not for the call', 'not for 2222' or any other number assigned for cardiopulmonary arrest emergency calls. The Resuscitation Council outlines situations when resuscitation is considered futile (BMA, 2002).

The first recorded attempt to administer resuscitation was around 800BC in Elijah's attempt to give a child 'mouth to mouth' (Bible, 2 Kings IV, 34–35). Mouth-to-mouth resuscitation was first attempted as early as 1950. Cardiopulmonary resuscitation was not then used in hospitals except to 'prevent premature death in previously "fit" patients, who sustained a sudden cardiac or respiratory arrest' (Levack, 2002, p.2). There are times when questions may be asked about the appropriateness of the use of cardiopulmonary resuscitation, especially if it is futile because of poor outcomes.

Healthcare professionals need a theoretical moral framework, such as 'principlism', to guide them in making ethical decisions when issues on end of life decisions may be related to a resuscitation status. There is debate as to whether a patient should be involved in decision-making related to their resuscitation status, and whether every patient's permission should be sought for doctors to initiate a 'non-resuscitation' status in a patient's notes. This could be interpreted as withdrawing treatment.

Case study

A 67-year-old cancer patient found she had had a 'DNR' order written on her medical notes without her consent. The patient saw that her notes had a 'do not resuscitate' entry from a previous admission. She complained she had not been consulted about this decision or options on whether she would like to be resuscitated. As it happened, the patient in question had a wish to be resuscitated in the event of a cardiac arrest ...: 'she was understandably distressed by this as no discussion had taken place with her or her next of kin,' said a doctor (BBC News, 27 June 2000).

A 'do not resuscitate' order can cause conflict and a breach of trust between the patient, family members and healthcare professionals (Beigler, 2003). Owing to threats of litigation, modern healthcare practice may develop a culture of defensive medicine, assuming that prior to every death, cardiopulmonary resuscitation should be pursued. Professional bodies have issued the guidelines *Decisions Relating to Cardiopulmonary Resuscitation*, as an example of joint work by the British Medical Association (BMA), the Resuscitation Council (UK) and the Royal College of Nursing (RCN). The BMA as well as related medical royal colleges and the RCN have all agreed on a code of practice (BMA, 1995) (see also the GMC (2006) *Guidance to Good Medical Practice*).

There are recent changes to the guidelines:

> *The overall clinical responsibility for decisions about cardiopulmonary resuscitation including DNAR decisions rests with the most senior clinician as defined by local policy. This could be a consultant, GP or suitably experienced nurse.*

> *BMA, 2007*

The Department of Health also requires clinical areas to have resuscitation policies 'which respect patients' rights in place, understood by all staff and accessible to those who need them, and that such policies are subject to appropriate audit and monitoring arrangements' (NHS Executive, 2000, p.1). Such a policy should be published locally for all interested parties.

It is important to involve family members in the decision-making (where possible to ascertain the patient's wishes), however, only the court may have the final decision on withdrawal of treatment. In cases where there is a diagnosis of persistent vegetative state (PVS) the state 'results from severe damage to the cerebral cortex, resulting in destruction of tissue in the thinking, feeling part of the brain. Patients appear awake but show no psychologically meaningful responses to stimuli and it is common for cerebral atrophy to occur. The condition is distinguished from a state of low awareness and the minimally conscious state (MCS) where patients show minimal but definite evidence of consciousness despite profound cognitive impairment' (BMA, 2006). The patient is required to have been in such a state for more than six months. It is the responsibility of the healthcare professionals to keep the family informed of any changes. The effect of any perceived or real shortcomings in the care of their loved ones may adversely affect them as, 'the harm you do in depriving someone of something that they can value ... you may also wrong those who care about them' (Keon, 1997, p.9).

Healthcare professionals and the next of kin can agree to withdraw treatment or not to initiate new active treatment, provided this is in the patient's best interest. When there is disagreement between healthcare professionals and family members, the case should be referred to the courts. By carrying out inappropriate treatment there is a danger of raising the hopes of family members close to the patient without achieving much. The most difficult moment for both healthcare professionals and the family members is likely to be when a decision to withdraw treatment must be made. This has to be done when it is obvious that despite acute interventions, the patient is going to die, and the treatment is said to be futile. Winter and Cohen (1999) observe that there are difficulties in justifying the use of the term 'relative futile' in respect of such treatment. It is dangerous as it introduces an unknown and potentially variable factor – namely the doctor's judgement (Winter and Cohen, 1999, p.3). That judgement may turn out to be wrong as in the following case.

Glass v United Kingdom (2004) (application no. 61827/00)

The case followed the admission of a patient, a child who suffered from learning disabilities, who was in a poorly state suffering from a chest infection. He was represented by his mother as guardian who sued the Trust because doctors had made the decision to treat the patient and place a 'do not attempt resuscitation order' above his bed and started a diamorphine pump. This was all done without consulting his mother. A physical fight ensued during which several police officers and two doctors were injured. His mother nevertheless wanted his treatment continued. The court held unanimously in favour of the patient on the basis that the Trust had been in breach of Article 8 (right to respect for private life) of the European Convention on Human Rights 1998.

This point on the validity of DNAR orders is highlighted in the following case.

> ### Re R (Adults: Medical Treatment) (1996) 31 BMLR 127
>
> A 23-year-old man, who was born with brain damage, had multiple medical problems which included having developed epilepsy as a child. Unable to communicate, he appeared to be constantly in considerable acute pain. He was however, conscious, having required constant care in a nursing home for the previous four years with weekend respite care, and he had been in and out of hospital with various ailments. There had been an agreement between the family and doctors that he should not be a candidate for active resuscitation. The Trust, however, sought a declaration on withdrawal of treatment. It was held by Sir Stephen Brown that the 'do not resuscitate' order was lawful, on the basis that in cases where cardiopulmonary resuscitation was unlikely to succeed, this could be justified.

Scottish law (*Law Hospital NHS Trust* v *Lord Advocate* [1996] 2 FLR 407) inclines towards a different approach in favour of withdrawal of treatment. However, the GMC's Withholding and Withdrawing Life Prolonging Treatments (GMC, 2002, paragraph 16) requires that, in the first place, 'doctors must take account of patients' preferences when providing treatment. However where a patient wishes to have a treatment that in the doctor's considered view is not clinically indicated, there is no ethical or legal obligation on the part of the doctor to provide it'. Difficulties may arise when family members disagree with the decision to continue treatment as illustrated in the following case.

> ### W Healthcare NHS Trust v H [2005] I WLR 834
>
> A nasogastric feeding tube for a 59-year-old MS patient fell out. The patient was conscious but had lacked mental capacity for decision-making having been on tube feeding for five years prior to this. The family objected to the tube being reinserted. It was held by the court that in the absence of a valid advance directive, it was in the patient's best interest for the tube to be reinserted.

PERSISTENT VEGETATIVE STATE

A suitable definition for PVS is

> *A person who has lost cognitive neurological function, meaning that the upper part of the brain that controls the more sophisticated functions*

such as speech, movement and thought, has died. People in PVS are able to breathe unaided as the lower part of the brain (the brain stem) is still functioning.

NHS Direct Online Health
Encyclopaedia (2002)

It is important to distinguish between PVS and a comatose state. In the case of the former, the condition is scientifically irrecoverable once the harm is done. If a patient is in a coma there is a chance of recovery. The Royal College of Physicians acknowledged that 'any diagnosis of PVS is not absolute but based on probability' (Royal College of Physicians, 1996, pp.119–21). In the case of a patient in a PVS who may be on a ventilator, the withdrawal of treatment must be more formal and guidelines set out by the BMA and the GMC should always be followed (see *Bolam* v *Friern Hospital Management Committee* [1957] 1 WLR 582). There may be difficulties in establishing the criteria as PVS stems from the distinction between a 'brain stem' death where there is loss of neurological functions and evidence of basic life and a biological death (Campbell *et al.*, 2001).

A patient who is being fed by artificial means may be considered alive only in the most basic of the biological or vegetative sense if they are deprived of brain function. It is believed that the true sense of death means that 'the brainstem concept of death means that death does not occur until both the brain as a whole and the body as a whole are irreversibly dysfunctional' (Campbell *et al.*, 2001, p.197). The brain damage must be so severe that the condition cannot be reversed. Ongoing expensive treatment raises questions about how far medical science should go to sustain a 'brain dead' patient.

Some view sustaining these patients' lives as unethical because of its expense. Still others centre the debate on whether or not PVS patients are persons. If not, they see no obligation to continue providing food and fluids. Others propose resolving this dilemma by creating new criteria for determining when death occurs. If PVS patients are actually dead, there should be little argument over withholding or withdrawing their food and fluids.

O'Mathuna, www.nhsdirect.nhs.uk

A patient is regarded as having been in PVS or a condition closely resembling PVS if this has persisted for at least six months. In England and Wales a court order to withdraw treatment should be sought for a review (BMA, 2003).

Artificial nutrition and hydration from a patient in PVS ... the judgment made it clear that it was not necessary to apply to the courts in every case where withdrawal of artificial nutrition and hydration is proposed from a patient with PVS.

BMA (2000, p.2)

THINKING POINT

John, a 25-year-old single young man who was a successful accountant in the City, suffered head and multiple injuries in a car crash about four weeks prior to admission to hospital. He was the only child of a middle-aged couple. He had undergone two surgical procedures to remove a blood clot following a sub-dural haemorrhage and returned to the Intensive Care Unit. He had not made any significant improvement since the last operation and had in fact suffered from a stroke and resulting brain stem damage. Over the following week post-operatively, his general condition steadily deteriorated, the prognosis is poor and his family are obviously devastated by the news.

A week later, the consultant physician responsible for John's care advised the parents that their son was not making any progress, and that he was now in a PVS having been an inpatient for the last six and a half months in the High Dependency Unit. The consultant discusses discontinuing treatment with the family, who disagree.

Consider the ethical and legal issues in the above scenario.

LIVING WILLS/ADVANCE DIRECTIVES AND THE RIGHT TO CHOOSE

Advance directives are a patient's formal instructions on their wishes to refuse certain specified treatment should their condition deteriorate. They may only be used as an indication of treatment a patient may choose to decline, not as a basis for demanding certain forms of treatment. An advance refusal of treatment is defined as

A refusal made by a person aged eighteen or over with the necessary capacity of any medical, surgical or dental treatment or other proced-ure and intended to have effect at any subsequent time when he or she may be without capacity to refuse consent.

The Law Commission (1995)

Living wills are the physical evidence of a patient's wishes should their con-dition deteriorate and they are too incapacitated to indicate their wishes. Similar arrangements are now in place in England and Wales (Sections 24–26, Mental Capacity Act 2005) following Scotland (Adults with Incapacity (Scotland) Act 2000), where a healthcare proxy document is used to describe either a living will or the full power granted to a proxy to make decisions on the patient's behalf. In the case of *Airedale NHS Trust* v *Bland* [1993] I ALL ER 821 HL, Lord Goff, at 872, in particular said that the courts would reject the 'substituted judgment test', which means the court will not recognize any decision on the basis of informal arrangements for proxy decision-making.

The Law Commission report on mental incapacity (Law Commission, 1995) recommended acceptance of any advance 'refusals' of consent to treatment as well as the principle of patient autonomy. This recognizes human rights for patients and includes the right to accept or refuse treatment.

Since the ruling in *Airedale Trust* v *Bland* [1993], living wills have been recognized as evidence of 'the patient's wish' to limit or to refuse treatment. Any will drawn up prior to a patient's deterioration must satisfy the above prerequisites, and for the will to have legal validity must originate from a person who is of competent mind.

The essential elements of a living will are similar to an ordinary will in Trust law. They are based on the BMA 1995 code of practice on advance directives (Dimond, 2002):

- full name;
- address;
- name and address of next of kin;
- whether advice was sought from health professionals;
- signature;
- date drafted and reviewed;
- witness signature;
- a clear statement of patient's wishes;
- name, address and telephone of nominated person.

From October 2007, living wills may now be recognized in law related to treatment decisions following the passing of the Mental Capacity Act 2005, with Sections 24–26 dealing with advance directives:

> *Advance decisions to refuse treatment: general*
>
> 24. (1) *'Advance decision' means a decision made by a person ('P'), after he has reached 18 and when he has capacity to do so, that if*
>
> (a) *at a later time and in such circumstances as he may specify, a specified treatment is proposed to be carried out or continued by a person providing healthcare for him, and*
>
> (b) *at that time he lacks capacity to consent to the carrying out or continuation of the treatment.*
>
> **Mental Capacity Act 2005**

Assessment of a patient's mental incapacity should be based on what is called the 'functional approach', based on the common law. This depends on whether at the time of decision the patient is:

> *(1) Unable by reason of mental disability to make a decision on the matter in question or,*
> *(2) Unable to communicate a decision on that matter because he or she is unconscious or for any other reason.*
>
> **Law Commission (1999, paragraph 3, 14)**

In the event of the absence of a living will, a doctor is obliged to act in the patient's best interests in light of any evidence of the patient's previously expressed wishes (Section 4 of the Mental Capacity Act 2005). The case of Burke (discussed above) illustrates this point.

Incapacity may be temporary or permanent. Caring for an unconscious or PVS patient can be a stressful experience and a dilemma for the healthcare professional under whose care the patient is entrusted (Brazier, 2003). The American lawyer Louis Kutner is credited with the concept of 'living wills' in 1969, arguing that 'the legal trust established over property should be equally permissible and applicable to one's body' and emphasizing 'the importance of consent or withholding consent to treatment, whatever the prospect of recovery' (Kendrick and Robinson, 2002, p.39).

If all the criteria for drawing up living wills are met, they should serve as valid evidence for either giving a direction as to what treatment to accept or what treatment to refuse (*Nursing Times*, 1999). Two consultants may give consent on behalf of an incapacitated patient in an emergency (Department of Health, 2001). Family members should be consulted only to establish the patient's best interests but not give consent on behalf of an incapacitated patient. If family members are not happy with a decision made by clinicians they have no right under the law to overrule that decision but can seek a judicial review. Doctors, however, do not have to follow these directives if this is not in keeping with their training and their conscience; they are entitled to seek a second medical opinion if they disagree with the proxy.

THE DOUBLE EFFECT DOCTRINE AND PALLIATIVE CARE

The double effect doctrine is that where death is an unintended outcome, a positive act such as analgesia control (which is legitimate but may hasten the death of the patient) is lawful. This principle was first developed in the following case.

R v *Bodkin-Adams* [1956] Crim LR (UK) 365

An elderly patient suffered a stroke and the doctor (who happened to be a substantial beneficiary of the victim's will) decided to increase the opiate analgesic and the patient died. It was held that he was not guilty of murder if the first objective of medicine, restoration of health, was successful and if the practice was backed by a responsible body of professionals.

Healthcare professionals have a duty of care in law and under the ethical principle of non-malevolence to ensure that patients have adequate and appropriate pain control and not to overmedicate a patient. Their primary aim should be to achieve the right balance for pain control. In the above case, it was held further by Lord Devlin that 'a doctor can do all that is proper and necessary to relieve pain and suffering, even if the measures he takes incidentally shorten life'. The World Health Organization defines palliative care as:

> *Palliative care is an approach which improves the quality of life of patients and their families facing life-threatening illness, through the prevention, assessment and treatment of pain and other physical, psychosocial and spiritual problems. The goal of palliative care is achievement of the best possible quality of life for patients and their families.*
>
> ### Houses of Parliament Health Committee (2004)

When a patient is in pain, it can be difficult to ascertain their true needs if their declared request is an indication of a preference for 'euthanasia' saying they would like to 'end it all' or if, in fact, this may be an indication of their frustration and an expression of pain. It is possible that as soon as the pain is relieved, a patient will be a very different person and they may express a wish to be discharged and/or to live a little longer. The nurse then faces a dilemma in ascertaining the patient's needs.

It is possible that a patient's wish 'to end it all' may be motivated by unbearable pain and/or poor pain control, or simply because they miss a loved one who has died before them. If the pain becomes insufferable then they may see death as the only way out and a welcome relief.

THINKING POINT

Peter, a 94-year-old man who is a retired district judge, is in the advanced stages of lung cancer with secondary metastases in the spine. He had been happily married for 69 years. Although not religious, he has been a humanist. He is now unconscious most of the time and the medication he is on makes

(Continued)

him drowsy and unable to respond to conversation although he is aware of the presence of his family and responds to his 86-year-old wife's voice. He had apparently informed one of his four sons, Y, who like him is a member of a society which promotes euthanasia, that he has no wish to live in view of his condition and of the unbearable pain. The son claiming to represent his father's wishes insists that antibiotic treatment for a chest infection should be stopped. The rest of the family however disagree and demand that because of their cultural and religious beliefs he should be treated with all available medicines until the very end (even if it will make no change to his long-term prognosis). The patient himself is unaware of the ensuing conflict of interests. The multidisciplinary team suggests palliative care and the family accept the outcome.

What role should the nurse play in supporting the patient and his family?

The courts in the UK are clear about their reluctance to extend the law on euthanasia as is clear in the following case.

A National Health Service Trust v *D* ([2000] FCR 577)

This case considered the right to resuscitation of a 19-month-old severely disabled child. The medical staff decided not to give him active treatment due to an expected short life expectancy. It was held, that 'the court's clear respect for the sanctity of human life must impose a strong obligation in favour of taking all steps capable of preserving life, save in exceptional circumstances'. The court took the view that withholding life-prolonging treatment did not breach Article 2 and that the primary consideration should not be the views of the family members or friends of the patient. Any clinical decision on the course of action to be followed should be based on the patient's best interests. Mr Justice Cazalet observed that 'there does not appear to be a decision of the European Court which indicates that the approach adopted by the English courts in situations such as this is contrary to Article 2'.

The court also acknowledged that the relevant consideration in treating the patient was not the doctors' views but the patient's best interest in relieving pain symptoms, albeit knowing that the side effect would be the hastening of death.

THE SLIPPERY SLOPE – CROSSING THE RUBICON

The common law makes no distinction between active measures and passive omissions, which may result in harm and breach of duty of care for a patient to have grounds for action in tort.

The cases of *Donaghue* v *Stevenson* [1932] and subsequently *Caparo Industries* v *Dickman* [1990] in Chapter 1 define the duty of care.

Difficulties may be posed in the decision-making process and in setting a precedent when dealing with grey areas and the danger of 'crossing the Rubicon' (Tony Bland case, see Brazier, 2003). When conflicts arise, judges, who must make decisions during judicial reviews seeking clarification on end of life decisions, must take into account the morals of society, which shapes their own ethical considerations. The law is not always clear-cut and a lot depends on whether there is some agreement with family members on whether to continue treatment. With any decision that allows the end of life, it is possible that some will see this as cheapening life, which must be preserved at all costs, while some may consider this a human right to be allowed to die with dignity.

On the other hand, criminal law is very clear on the elements of murder. The *mens rea* (criminal intent) can be established as well as the *actus reus* (guilty act). This cannot be the case when withdrawal is the only option, when it is agreed by the multidisciplinary team that in the patient's best interests, further treatment would be futile, 'both medically and ethically, in the face of overwhelming disease' (Cohen, 1993, p.52).

Finally, it is useful to describe briefly how euthanasia has been received in other countries. Australia's Northern Territory passed the Natural Death Act, which came into effect in July 1996, allowing euthanasia. It was in operation for less than a year (when four people were allowed to commit physician suicide) before it was repealed by the federal government of Australia. In the USA, all states apart from Oregon do not allow euthanasia. The Netherlands is of particular interest because of its liberal views on euthanasia. It has strict guidelines with conditions to be met as follows:

(a) *The request must come from the patient. It must, in addition be free and voluntary.*

(b) *This request must have been a considered and persistent one.*

(c) *The patient should be suffering intolerably ... there should be no prospect for improvement.*

(d) *The decision to end the patient's life must be one of the last resort having considered whether there is any less drastic alternative.*

(e) *The euthanasia must be performed by a doctor who has beforehand consulted with an independent doctor who has experience in the area of euthanasia.*

Davies (1998, p.352)

The Dutch practice of euthanasia was formalized by legislation in 2000 to allow both physician-assisted euthanasia and assisted suicide. Official figures showed there was a significant increase (from 16 per cent to 41 per cent of deaths) in euthanasia between 1990 and 1995 (Hendin, 2002, p.2). The level of Dutch tolerance of euthanasia is demonstrated in the following case.

Case study

In 1985, a doctor was charged with being implicated in about 20 deaths in a nursing home, without the knowledge or consent of the victims. He was found guilty and sentenced to a year in prison but, following an outcry against the severity of the sentence, the verdict was overturned on a technicality. He was then awarded the equivalent of US$150 000 damages by a civil court.

Pollard (2004)

The Dutch system has been criticized for failing to protect vulnerable patients and to address patients' choice and their right to autonomy, by failing to obtain proper and informed consent prior to euthanasia in more than 1000 cases (Hendin, 2002). The worrying factor here is that it is almost impossible to tell the real levels of such cases, as this is difficult to monitor and to establish doctors' compliance with the guidelines. Similarly, other European countries such as Switzerland and Belgium have followed suit in legitimizing physician-assisted euthanasia.

The Select Committee on Medical Ethics (Walton Committee (1994), House of Lords, 1993–94, paragraph 260) drew a line on morality, which they felt reflected the feelings of the majority of the UK public, and refused to extend the law by 'crossing the line which prohibits any intentional killing, a line which we think it is essential to preserve'. They suggested further that it was important that the move to block the legitimization of 'intentional killing' was seen 'as the cornerstone of law and the social relationships' (House of Lords Paper 21-1, 1993–94). Where there is a lack of clarity or dispute, a judicial review should always be sought in order to safeguard patient rights. The law as it stands in the UK is based on the rule in *Airedale NHS Trust* v *Bland* [1993], where Lord Goff (at 870–871) observed that artificial feeding and hydration should only be discontinued when the condition was deemed to be permanent and in the patient's best interests. He went on to demonstrate his dilemma in balancing continuing treatment against stopping.

> *But it is not lawful for a doctor to administer a drug even though that course is prompted by humanitarian desire to end his suffering, however great that suffering may be.*

Furthermore, there is a need for balancing the patient's needs for pain control and their interest in being put through what can only be seen as burdensome treatment.

> *So to cross the Rubicon which runs between, on the one hand, the care of the living patient and on the other hand euthanasia actively causing his death to avoid or to end his suffering. Euthanasia is not lawful at Common Law.*
>
> **Airedale NHS Trust *v* Bland [1993]**

There are real difficulties for doctors in determining the motivation for a patient's request for 'euthanasia', which could be linked to depression.

> *In terminally ill patients, depression often fluctuates with pain, as well as altering the perception of the pain and subjective views of the future. The desire to die has been found to decrease over time in terminally ill persons (Chochinov et al., 1995). Specifically, the wish for euthanasia or PAS changes over time in a large proportion of terminally ill patients, and decision instability is particularly associated with depressive symptoms (Emanuel et al., 2000).*
>
> **Statement from the Royal College of Psychiatrists on Physician Assisted Suicide**

It is difficult to establish the number of cases of euthanasia although UK research involving general practitioners has suggested a figure of 584 791 deaths in England, Wales, Scotland and Northern Ireland. The most significant areas were alleviation of symptoms with possible life shortening (32.8 per cent) and non-treatment decisions (30.3 per cent). No voluntary euthanasia was recorded. Some have suggested that since its initiation as many as 453 people including 30 from the UK, have been given assisted euthanasia through Dignitas, in Switzerland (LifeSite, 2005). The danger of organizations such as Dignitas is that the motivation for ending life may be other than an intolerable suffering due to a medical condition as in the case reported by Leidig (2005).

CONCLUSION

Similar to healthcare professionals, judges may also face a dilemma in dealing with end of life decisions. There are often grey areas and ethical decisions, which are fraught with difficulties, as judges follow their own ethics.

> *The conclusion I have reached will appear to some to be almost irrational. How can it be lawful to allow a patient to die slowly though painlessly over a period of weeks from lack of food, but unlawful to*

produce his immediate death by a lethal injection, thereby saving his family from yet another ordeal? (Furthermore) … I find it difficult to find a moral answer to that question. But it is undoubtedly the law.

Lord Browne-Wilkinson, Tony Bland v Airedale NHS Trust [1993]

Healthcare professionals, on the one hand, should act as representatives of their respective professional bodies and as advocates of patients who have no one to look after their interests. Sometimes a dilemma becomes a conflict of interests as they wrestle with their conscience. The courts, on the other hand, have the opportunity to bring in changes by the back door by widening the interpretation of the legislation as intended by parliament. The European Court of Human Rights may strike down any UK judgements that appear to contravene human rights legislation.

The role of ethics is to provide frameworks that are based on custom and human knowledge, which is fallible and has been subject to change at different times in history. Is it possible then that as a society we in the UK are becoming more and more indifferent to the value of human life and turning a blind eye to our innate conscience? Some philosophers like Kant (1724–1804) believed that ignoring our 'categorical imperative' to preserve life would be immoral. The utilitarian view would make end of life decisions on the basis of usefulness to the majority in society rather than the best interests of the patient, thus there is a possibility of making individual autonomy meaningless and some patients vulnerable (*R* v *Bodkin-Adams* [1956]). This could mean the easy way out – 'people just being written off by the system' (*Daily Telegraph*, 1999, p.11).

There is no clear evidence that in countries where euthanasia is legal the link between depression and requests for euthanasia is taken into consideration. The ethical values of any given nation are influenced by moral philosophy and religious values, which may influence decisions, 'these are remarkably durable in the sense that their influence spans over the centuries' (Elford, 2000, p.13). Values that may conflict even within a given society or internationally are difficult to change overnight. There is so far no persuasive evidence to convince the public and the healthcare professional bodies in the UK that the interests of the patient would be best served by widening the category of patients eligible for euthanasia. The UK parliament does not so far support changing the status quo. One dilemma facing any healthcare professional involved in end of life decisions is that, even in the case of a patient whose has the capacity to make a decision, they may never be able to say with certainty whether or not a request for 'euthanasia' is a cry for help.

A balance should be struck between how best to serve the patient's interests, while fulfilling the healthcare professional's own personal conscience as well as following professional guidelines (within the constraints of the law). The Law Commission on Mental Incapacity suggested that:

> *One of the principles on which the Commission has proceeded is that people should be encouraged and enabled to take those decisions which they are in fact able to take. This principle embraces anticipatory decision-making by the person while competent in order to make arrangements for his or her future incapacity.*
> **Law Commission (1995, Paragraph 1.12)**

There may be real difficulties in family members or a healthcare proxy or deputy accurately reflecting the wishes of the patient if they themselves have vested interests in inheritance, which is a motive in criminal law. Lord Joffe's 'The Patient Assisted Dying Bill' has been one attempt by a private member in the House of Lords to change the law by legalizing euthanasia with a provision for opting out for conscientious objectors as well a chance for a competent patient's considered decision. The debate on end of life decisions goes on.

REFERENCES

BBC News. 27 June 2000, http://news.bbc.co.uk.

Beauchamp TL, Childress J. *Principles of biomedical ethics*. New York: Oxford University Press, 1997.

Beigler P. Should patient consent be required to write a do not resuscitate order? *Journal of Medical Ethics* 2003; **29**: 359–63.

BMA. *Advance statements about medical treatment: Code of practice with explanatory notes*. London: BMJ Publishing Group, 1995.

BMA. *Withholding life prolonging medical treatment: Guidance for decision making*. London: BMJ Publishing Group, 2000, www.bma.org.uk/ap.nsf/content/withholdingwithdrawing, 3rd edition, 2007.

BMA. *Decisions relating to cardiopulmonary resuscitation. A joint statement from the British Medical Association, the Resuscitation Council (UK) and the Royal College of Nursing*. London: British Medical Association, 2002.

BMA. 2003. www.bma.org.uk/ap.nsf/content/home, accessed 15/1/07.

BMA. Paragraph 13, p. 19, *Decisions relating to cardiopulmonary resuscitation. A joint statement from the BMA, the Resuscitation Council (UK) and the RCN*. London: British Medical Association, 2007. www.bma.org.uk, accessed 10/11/2007.

BMA. *Guidelines on treatment decisions for patients in persistent vegetative state*. Revised December 2006, http://www.bma.org.uk/ap.nsf/Content/pvstreatment#ref.

Brazier M. *Medicine, patients and the law*. London: Penguin, 2003.

Butterworths. *Butterworths' student statutes*, 2nd edn. London: Butterworths, 2000.

Campbell A, Gillett G, Jones G. *Medical ethics*, 3rd edn. Oxford: Oxford University Press, 2001.

Cohen S. *Whose life is it anyhow?* London: Robson Books,1993.

Davies M. *Medical law*, 2nd edn. London: Blackstone Press, 1998.

Department of Health. *Resuscitation policy*. Health Service Circular, 2000, HSC 2000/028.

Department of Health. *Consent – What you have a right to expect: a guide for adults*. 2001, www.dh.gov.uk/en/Policyandguidance/Healthandsocial caretopics/Consent/Consentgeneralinformation/index.htm.

Dimond B. *Legal aspects of pain management*. British Journal of Nursing Monograph. Dinton: Quay Books, 2002.

Dyer C. Court test for a new legal rights, *Guardian*, 2 October 2000.

EC Human Rights Commission. 1991, quoted by the Church of Scotland, Social Work *Euthanasia, a church perspective*. Edinburgh: St Andrews Press, 1995.

Elford RJ. *The ethics of uncertainty*. Oxford: One World, 2000.

General Medical Council. *Withholding and withdrawing life prolonging treatments*. 2002, paragraph 16, www.gmc-uk.org.

General Medical Council. *Guidance to good medical practice*. 2006, www.gmc-uk.org/guidance/good_medical_practice/index.asp.

Hendin H. *Practice versus theory, the Dutch experience*. Houston, TX: International Association for Hospices and Palliative Care, 2002, www.hospicecare.com/AOM/2002/mar2002article.htm.

House of Lords/ Paper 21 of 21-1 of 1993–94 paragraph 260.

Houses of Parliament Health Committee. 2004. www.publications. parliament.uk/pa/cm200304/cmselect/cmhealth/454/454.pdf, accessed 15/11/07.

Kant I. *Fundamental principles in metaphysics of morals*. New York: Liberal Arts Press, 1785.

Kendrick K, Robinson S. *Their rights, advance directives and living wills explored*. London: Age Concern, 2002.

Keon J. *Euthanasia examined, ethical clinical and legal perspective*. Cambridge: Cambridge University Press, 1997.

Kubler-Ross E. *On life after death*. Berkeley, CA: Celestial Arts, 1991.

Law Commission. *The Law Commission Report on Mental Incapacity*. 1995, (LC231), www.lawcom.gov.uk.

Lefroy V, Hammond H. *Study into euthanasia and end-of-life decisions*. 2004, www.brunel.ac.uk/news/pressoffice/cdata/euthanasia.

Leidig M. Dignitas is investigated for helping healthy woman to die, *BMJ* 2005; **331**:1160.

Levack P. Live and let die? A structured approach to decision making about resuscitation. *British Journal of Anaesthesia* 2002; **89**: 683–6.

LifeSite. Swiss euthanasia group Dignitas opening British office. 2005, www.lifesite.net/ldn/2005/oct/05101103.html.

Lord Joffe. *Assisted dying for the terminally ill*. [HL] Vol. II, HL Paper 86-2, 2005.

Morgan P, Lawton P. *Ethical issues in six religious traditions*. Edinburgh: Edinburgh University Press, 1996.

NHS Direct. Online Health Encyclopaedia. 2002, www.nhsdirect.nhs.uk.

NHS Executive. *Resuscitation policy*. London: Department of Health, 2000 (HSC 2000/028).

Nursing Times. Nursing Times essential guides: living wills. London, EMAP Healthcare, 1999.

O'Mathuna P. *Responding to patients in the persistent vegetative state*. www.xenos. org.org/ministries/crossroads/donal/pvs.htm.

Pollard B. *Euthanasia practices in the Netherlands*. www.catholiceducation. org/articles/euthanasia/eu0014.html, accessed 09/09/04.

Royal College of Psychiatrists. Response to Assisted Dying for the Terminally Ill Bill, 24 April 2006, http://www.rcpsych.ac.uk/press parliament/collegeresponses/physicianassistedsuicide.aspx?theme= print.

Royal College of Physicians. The permanent vegetative state. Review by a working group convened by the Royal College of Physicians and endorsed by the Conference of Medical Royal Colleges and their faculties of the United Kingdom. *Journal of the Royal College of Physicians of London* 1996; **30**:119–21.

Teichman J. *Social ethics, a student's guide*. Oxford: Blackwell Publishers, 1996.

Viney C. A phenomenological study of ethical decision-making experiences among senior intensive care nurses and doctors concerning withdrawal of treatment. *Nursing in Critical Care* 1996; **1**: 182–7.

Winter B, Cohen S. Withdrawal of treatment. ABC of intensive treatment. *BMJ* 1999; **319**: 306–8.

10 HUMAN RIGHTS AND PATIENT CARE

PATERNALISM AND PATIENTS' RIGHTS

The Hippocratic oath appears to underpin the biomedical model of care (which prefers to focus on restoration of a patient's biological functioning but not on the psychosocial aspect, giving a patient their own individuality and autonomy). Patient preferences of this model were supported by research by Arora and McHorney (2000), who reported that, given the choice, 69 per cent of patients preferred to leave decision-making to their doctor. It is possible that paternalism could leave patients' rights open to abuse by healthcare professionals. This would mean that patient autonomy and informed consent, which should be central to provision of care, would not be taken into consideration. In paternalism, there is no room for a partnership with patients concerning decisions about their own treatment. Paternalism was synonymous with blind 'trust' in doctors and other healthcare professionals such as nurses. The problem, however, was that without any guarantees of patients' rights that trust could be breached when making clinical decisions.

The modern view of this relationship needs to consider the patient's psychosocial needs and sees nursing as now based on

> *The use of clinical judgment in the provision of care to enable people to improve, maintain, or recover health, to cope with health problems, and to achieve the best possible quality of life, whatever their disease or disability, until death.*
>
> ***Royal College of Nursing (2003)***

Most patients are now aware of their human rights. It may be more difficult for healthcare professionals to safeguard the patient's rights when a patient lacks mental capacity for decision-making. When the law is unclear the nurse must always consult professional colleagues in acting 'in the patient's best interests'.

Nursing has emerged as a profession alongside medicine and is largely supportive of it, reinforcing the notion that only doctors were qualified to make decisions on treatment – patient involvement was not considered important. In the past, the doctor played the crucial role of making unilateral decisions on treatment while nurses were expected to fulfil an ancillary role in carrying out the doctor's orders. The patient, on the other hand, was not expected to voice any opinion or to be involved in decision-making. Patients' rights were not always recognized. Human rights were in danger of being ignored on the basis that the doctor knew what was best for their patients. Today, nurses are increasingly taking on medical (extended) roles, with the accountability that comes with it and playing a central part in the provision of care.

HUMAN RIGHTS, LITIGATION AND PATIENTS

The emergence of modern medical science in the western world also meant the development of treatment into hitherto unknown territory. An often quoted American case, which is persuasive although not authoritative in the UK, defined a patient's common law rights:

> *Every person of adult years and sound mind has a right to determine what shall be done with his own body.*
> **Schloendorff *v* The Society of New York Hospital,**
> *211 NY 125,105, NE 92 [1914]*

Paternalism was a by-product of the progress in medical science. It was accepted as the norm not only by doctors but also nurses and other healthcare professionals. Unfortunately the implication of this was that patients were not expected to question medical decisions on their treatment and consequently it was possible that their human rights could be abused.

Since the implementation of the Human Rights Act (HRA) 1998 (in October 2000), patients have become increasingly aware of their human rights. Although it may not necessarily be linked, there has been an increase in complaints with the UK becoming a more litigious society. In 2005–06, there were 5697 claims of clinical negligence and 3497 claims of non-clinical negligence against the NHS, a small increase on the previous period, with £560.3 million having been paid out for clinical negligence claims for the same period (NHS Litigation Authority, 2007).

Human rights as contained in Schedule 1 of the HRA 1998 are the embodiment of the European Convention on Human Rights 1950, which originated from the Universal Declaration of Human Rights 1948, which was a declaration of the United Nations on 10 December 1948. The UK, in 1953, was one of the first countries to ratify the European Convention although this was not legally enforceable in UK courts until the passing of the HRA 1998. The statute took effect from October 2000.

The basic tenets of human rights are found in the HRA 1998, Schedule 1 (BMA, 2007) and only those relevant to healthcare are summarized here as follows:

> *Principle 1*
> *Fundamental freedoms and basic rights*
>
> *1. All persons have the right to the best available mental health care, which shall be part of the health and social care system.*
>
> *Principles for the protection of persons with mental illness and the improvement of mental health care.*
> **United Nations General Assembly (1991)**

Article 2 – Right to life
Article 3 – Prohibition to torture
Article 4 – Prohibition of slavery and forced labour
Article 5 – Right to liberty and security
Article 6 – Right to a fair trial
Article 7 – No punishment without the law
Article 8 – Right to respect for private and family life
Article 9 – Freedom of expression
Article 10 – Freedom of expression
Article 12 – Right to marry and a family
Article 14 – Prohibition of discrimination

To reinforce the classification of these articles as discussed in Chapter 1, Aspects of law and human rights, the principles of human rights are usually subdivided into the following categories (Department of Constitutional Affairs, 2006):

- absolute;
- limited;
- qualified rights.

Individual patients with capacity should be allowed to make decisions which have an effect on their own treatment as well as their lives, especially those with continuing care needs.

Examples of public authorities who come under the jurisdiction of the HRA 1998 include local authorities, NHS Trusts, the police, prison and the Immigration Service. In reality, there are always difficulties for the patient in identifying evidence where their welfare is endangered by healthcare professionals' conduct. Most patients receiving healthcare are vulnerable and may lack physical or mental capacity. Patients may not have the energy to ensure that their rights are honoured and to fight against infringement of these rights, when recovery should be their primary concern.

The post-Second World War era brought to the forefront the issue of human rights and how best they should be protected in light of those who had perished because of the abuse of human rights.

The Declaration of Human Rights 1945 in Geneva recognized protection of human rights in general, but especially had vulnerable people such as patients in mind. Owing to their physical and mental condition many patients will fall into this category. Any person who is deemed to be a victim of a breach of human rights may bring an action under the Articles of the HRA 1998. UK courts have a duty to apply this legislation but a victim has the right of appeal to the European Court of Human Rights or they may lodge their case there instead if they so wish. It is recognized that the HRA has so far not managed to create a consensus of the law in specific areas (Mullally, 2006). What it has done is to generate a database of case law, which will be useful for victims of human rights' abuse. This resource will therefore facilitate the process of the application of human rights law (based on case law) in European Union member states.

The HRA 1998 has not altered, but enhanced, the substance of UK law in areas such as criminal law or employment law, where it has been able to benefit individuals in areas where interpretation of existing law lacked clarity or resulted in encroachment of human rights.

POLICY ISSUES – LOOKING AHEAD

The professional code of conduct and ethics now requires nurses to safeguard the patient's rights (NMC, 2004). From the legal perspective it is also clear that concerning patients' rights in the future, some cases may need to be tested in (through case law) some areas in order to ensure clarity. What is also certain is that human rights' legislation has had a direct impact on NHS policy formation, as Trusts must take on board its provisions in improving healthcare. One way this can be achieved is through education and training as well as by improving Trust policies and guidelines in areas such as resuscitation and dealing with patients' property.

> *The government remains fully committed to the European Convention on Human Rights, and to the way in which it is given effect in UK law by the Human Rights Act.*
> **Department of Constitutional Affairs (2006, p.1)**

CONCLUSION

It is recognized that the application of human rights legislation should be about improving public services including healthcare provision. It should also aim to rally the different branches of law to focus on human rights principles. As part of recognizing human rights, the patient needs, where possible, to be given a sufficient degree of information before being expected to make an informed choice. A nurse providing care may find themselves in the position of safeguarding the patient's rights, especially for those lacking capacity. The NHS Plan (2000) aimed at improving the patient's welfare through the following principles:

- redress over cancelled operations;
- patients' forums and citizens' panels in every area;
- new national panel to advise on major reorganization of hospitals;
- stronger regulation of professional standards.

In this day and age one is likely to hear about the Patients' Charter when complaints are lodged. This was abolished in 2000, under the NHS Plan (for 10 years). It was an attempt to set benchmarks for standards of care to ensure patients' rights. In the world of litigation, the general public may now be seen as keen to capitalize on claims based on poor care. When considering patients' rights it cannot be overstated that it is essential that nurses are aware that patients do have rights and that should they suffer harm as a result of clinical negligence, then they may be entitled to recover damages against them, in tort. The danger, however, is that their relationship may be surrounded by defensive practice, destroying any trust. It is difficult to justify this approach from the professional and ethical perspective, as care of other patients may be compromised where healthcare professionals are 'overtreating' a patient as a countermeasure against potential litigation.

It is better to manage care on the basis of risk management. Under the Health and Safety at Work Act (HASAWA) 1974, this means that any potential risks or hazards are reported and managed properly before a patient is harmed. This applies to both the employer (Sections 2–5; for example Section 2(1) Ensure the health, safety and welfare of employees while at work) and employee under the HASAWA 1974:

Section 7 (a–b) It shall be the duty of every employee while at work:

(a) To take reasonable care for the health and safety of himself and others who may be affected by his acts or omissions at work.

(b) To co-operate with his employer or any other person, so far as is necessary, to enable his employer or other person to perform or comply with any requirement or duty imposed under a relevant statutory provision.

The National Patient Safety Agency (NPSA) was established by the UK government in July 2001 for the purposes of coordinating the efforts of NHS Trusts in the UK by reporting mishaps and problems affecting patient safety and thus allowing Trusts to learn from any mistakes. The NPSA monitors the reporting of mishaps and also tries to 'promote an open and fair culture in the NHS, encouraging all healthcare staff to report incidents without undue fear of personal reprimand'. It will then collect reports from throughout the country and initiate preventative measures.

Given that only a certain amount of progress has been made in taking on board human rights in order to ensure patients' rights are respected, questions may still be asked, whether, as a society, we still have some way to go in recognizing patient's rights when caring for them. Some common experiences of patients were cited as follows.

Not enough involvement in decisions
No-one to talk to about anxieties and concerns
Tests and/or treatments not clearly explained
Insufficient information for family/friends
Insufficient information about recovery
Department of Health (2001)

Unfortunately, given the reality of the situation, it may not always be possible to guarantee the patient's best interests because of human error and limited resources and there is always room for improvement.

REFERENCES

Arora K, McHorney C (2000) Patient preferences for medical decision making: who really wants to participate? *Medical Care* 2000; **38**: 335–41.

Department of Constitutional Affairs. *Making sense of human rights; a short introduction*. Crown Copyright, 2006, www.dca.gov.uk, accessed 30/04/07.

Department of Health. *The expert patient: a new approach to chronic disease management for the 21st century*. 2001 (paragraph 1.7), www.dh.gov.uk/ en/ Publicationsandstatistics/Publications/PublicationsPolicyAndGuidance/ DH_4006801, accessed 16/11/07.

Mullally S. *Gender, culture and human rights: reclaiming universalism*. Oxford: Hart Publishing, 2006.

National Health Service. *The NHS Plan*, 2000. www.nhsia.nhs.uk/nhsplan/ summary.htm, accessed 16/11/07.

National Health Service Litigation Authority. 2007, http://www.nhsla. com/home.htm, accessed 20/07/07.

National Patient Safety Agency. www.npsa.nhs.uk/, accessed 12/04/07.

NMC. *Code of professional conduct, standards for conduct, performance and ethics*. London: Nursing and Midwifery Council, 2004.

Royal College of Nursing. *Defining nursing*. London: Royal College of Nursing, 2003, www.rcn.org.uk, accessed 01/02/07.

United Nations General Assembly. *The protection of persons with mental illness and the improvement of mental health care*. Resolution 46/119, 17 December 1991, www.un.org/documents/ga/res/46/a46r119.htm.

INDEX